Imagining Punjab, Punjabi and Punjabiat in the Transnational Era

This book moves away from originary myths of region and identity that have dominated academic and mediatized representations of Punjab, a land-locked region divided between India and Pakistan after the Partition of 1947, and instead focuses on the role of the imagination in producing Punjab. It examines Punjab as an ethno-spatial, ethno-linguistic and ethno-cultural construct produced by the communities who dwell there, those who have left it, and those formed by new narratives of the region. By isolating imaginings of Punjab that are not centred on exclusivist regional, linguistic, sectarian or caste perspectives, contributions to this book propose the concept of *free-flowing cartographies* in relation to Punjab, which facilitate its imaginings as a geographical region, a social construct and a state of consciousness. The region is simultaneously imagined as a small place, a neighbourhood, a city, and a village, but also as performative practices and certain ways of doing things.

Through focusing on a number of Punjabi spaces and communities and engaging with Punjab as a geographical region, social construct and state of consciousness, the papers in the book hope to contribute to broader debates on transnationalism, postnationalism, micronationalism, and new identity narratives emerging in the twenty first century.

This book was originally published as a special issue of *South Asian Diaspora*.

Anjali Gera Roy is a Professor in the Department of Humanities and Social Sciences at the Indian Institute of Technology, Kharagpur, India. She has published widely on South Asian literary, cultural and diaspora studies. Her books include *Bhangra Moves: From Ludhiana to London and Beyond* (2010), *Travels of Bollywood Cinema: From Bombay to LA* (2012), *Magic of Bollywood: At Home and Abroad* (2012) and *Partitioned Lives: Narratives of Home, Displacement and Resettlement* (2008). Her new book, *Cinema of Enchantment: Perso-Arabic Genealogies of the Hindi Masala Film* will be published by Orient Blackswan in 2015.

Imagining Punjab, Punjabi and Punjabiat in the Transnational Era

Edited by
Anjali Gera Roy

LONDON AND NEW YORK

First published 2015 by Routledge

2 Park Square, Milton Park, Abingdon, Oxon OX14 4RN
711 Third Avenue, New York, NY 10017, USA

Routledge is an imprint of the Taylor & Francis Group, an informa business

First issued in paperback 2017

Copyright © 2015 Taylor & Francis

All rights reserved. No part of this book may be reprinted or reproduced or utilised in any form or by any electronic, mechanical, or other means, now known or hereafter invented, including photocopying and recording, or in any information storage or retrieval system, without permission in writing from the publishers.

Notice:
Product or corporate names may be trademarks or registered trademarks, and are used only for identification and explanation without intent to infringe.

British Library Cataloguing in Publication Data
A catalogue record for this book is available from the British Library

ISBN 13: 978-1-138-88675-9 (hbk)
ISBN 13: 978-1-138-08285-4 (pbk)

Typeset in Times New Roman
by RefineCatch Limited, Bungay, Suffolk

Publisher's Note
The publisher accepts responsibility for any inconsistencies that may have arisen during the conversion of this book from journal articles to book chapters, namely the possible inclusion of journal terminology.

Disclaimer
Every effort has been made to contact copyright holders for their permission to reprint material in this book. The publishers would be grateful to hear from any copyright holder who is not here acknowledged and will undertake to rectify any errors or omissions in future editions of this book.

Contents

Citation Information vii
Notes on Contributors ix

1. Introduction: Imagining Punjab and the Punjabi diaspora: after more than a century of Punjabi migration 1
   Anjali Gera Roy

2. 'The heart, stomach and backbone of Pakistan': Lahore in novels by Bapsi Sidhwa and Mohsin Hamid 5
   Claire Chambers

3. Culture shock on Southall Broadway: re-thinking 'second-generation' return through 'geographies of Punjabiness' 24
   Kaveri Qureshi

4. Punjabiyat and the music of Nusrat Fateh Ali Khan 41
   Virinder S. Kalra

5. Tracing Sufi influence in the works of contemporary Siraiki Poet, Riffat Abbas 55
   Nukhbah Taj Langah

6. Exiled in its own land: Diasporification of Punjabi in Punjab 71
   Abbas Zaidi

7. (Dis)honourable paradigms: a critical reading of *Provoked*, *Shame* and *Daughters of Shame* 87
   Shweta Kushal and Evangeline Manickam

Index 101

Citation Information

The chapters in this book were originally published in *South Asian Diaspora*, volume 6, issue 2 (September 2014). When citing this material, please use the original page numbering for each article, as follows:

Chapter 1
Introduction: Imagining Punjab and the Punjabi diaspora: after more than a century of Punjabi migration
Anjali Gera Roy
South Asian Diaspora, volume 6, issue 2 (September 2014) pp. 137–140

Chapter 2
'The heart, stomach and backbone of Pakistan': Lahore in novels by Bapsi Sidhwa and Mohsin Hamid
Claire Chambers
South Asian Diaspora, volume 6, issue 2 (September 2014) pp. 141–159

Chapter 3
Culture shock on Southall Broadway: re-thinking 'second-generation' return through 'geographies of Punjabiness'
Kaveri Qureshi
South Asian Diaspora, volume 6, issue 2 (September 2014) pp. 161–177

Chapter 4
Punjabiyat and the music of Nusrat Fateh Ali Khan
Virinder S. Kalra
South Asian Diaspora, volume 6, issue 2 (September 2014) pp. 179–192

Chapter 5
Tracing Sufi influence in the works of contemporary Siraiki Poet, Riffat Abbas
Nukhbah Taj Langah
South Asian Diaspora, volume 6, issue 2 (September 2014) pp. 193–208

Chapter 6
Exiled in its own land: Diasporification of Punjabi in Punjab
Abbas Zaidi
South Asian Diaspora, volume 6, issue 2 (September 2014) pp. 209–224

CITATION INFORMATION

Chapter 7
(Dis)honourable paradigms: a critical reading of Provoked, Shame *and* Daughters of Shame
Shweta Kushal and Evangeline Manickam
South Asian Diaspora, volume 6, issue 2 (September 2014) pp. 225–238

Please direct any queries you may have about the citations to
clsuk.permissions@cengage.com

Notes on Contributors

Claire Chambers is a Lecturer in Global Literature at the University of York, UK, where she researches and teaches modern writing from South Asia, the Arab world, and their diasporas. She is the author of *British Muslim Fictions: Interviews with Contemporary Writers*. She has published widely in such journals as *Postcolonial Text*, *Crossings* and *Contemporary Women's Writing*, and is co-editor of the *Journal of Commonwealth Literature*.

Virinder S. Kalra teaches at Manchester University, UK, and his research interests are diaspora, popular culture and racism. His latest book is *Sacred and Secular Musics: A Postcolonial Approach* (2014) which looks at kirtan, Qawwali and dharmic geet in East and West Punjab. His previous books include *Diaspora and Hybridity*, and the co-edited *State of Race*.

Shweta Kushal holds a doctorate in English Literature from the Department of Humanities and Social Sciences at the Indian Institute of Technology Madras, India. She works on intercultural spaces that migrants inhabit and the manner in which gender affects the experience of these spaces. Her work has been published in refereed international journals. Her research interests include related areas of partition literature, culture studies, film studies, ethnicity, race and identity.

Nukhbah Taj Langah is an academic, writer and political activist. Her research broadly focuses on postcolonial literature, South Asian literature/diaspora, cultural and translation studies and more specifically, Siraiki and ethnic literary expressions from Pakistan. Her publications include various articles and poetry translations in international journals and a book titled, *Poetry as Resistance: Islam & Ethnicity in Postcolonial Pakistan* (Routledge, 2011). This book focuses on the emergence and maturity of Siraiki as a political and ethnic identity, transforming literature produced in this language into a symbol of resistance. She is currently Associate Professor and Head of the Department of English at Forman Christian College University, Lahore, Pakistan.

Evangeline Manickam is Professor of English in the Department of Humanities and Social Sciences at the Indian Institute of Technology Madras, India. She has been Senior Fulbright Scholar at the University of Georgia, Athens, Georgia, USA, and Louisiana State University, Baton Rouge, Louisiana, USA, 1984–1985, and Fulbright Visiting Lecturer in South Asian and South Asian Diaspora Literature focusing on Punjabi Diaspora Writing and Film at the University of Hawaii, Manoa, Hawaii, USA, 2011.

Kaveri Qureshi is a Research Fellow at the University of Oxford, UK. She has research interests in the anthropology of the Pakistani and Indian Punjabi diaspora. Her research focuses on gendered life courses and family life, and she has also published on migration, transnationalism and diasporic politics.

Anjali Gera Roy is a Professor in the Department of Humanities and Social Sciences at the Indian Institute of Technology Kharagpur, India, who works on fiction, film and performance traditions of India, diasporas and Punjab. She is the author of *Cinema of Enchantment: Perso-Arabic Genealogies of the Hindi Masala Film* (Hyderabad: Orient Blackswan, forthcoming 2015) and *Bhangra Moves: From Ludhiana to London and Beyond* (Aldershot: Ashgate, 2010). She has edited *Magic of Bollywood: At Home and Abroad* (Delhi: Sage, 2012). She has also co-edited (with Chua Beng Huat) *Travels of Indian Cinema: From Bombay to LA* (Delhi: OUP, 2012) and (with Nandi Bhatia) *Partitioned Lives: Narratives of Home, Displacement and Resettlement* (Delhi: Pearson Longman, 2008). In addition, she has published 100 essays in literary, film and cultural studies.

Abbas Zaidi has taught academic writing, media genres, and journalism in various universities including Maqaurie University, University of Western Sydney, and the University of New South Wales. He is the author of *Two and a Half Words and Other Stories* (Savvy Press), and *Language Shift: Sociolinguistic Lives of Two Punjabi Generations in Brunei Darussalam* (Lahore: Classic Books).

INTRODUCTION

Imagining Punjab and the Punjabi diaspora: after more than a century of Punjabi migration

Anjali Gera Roy

Department of Humanities & Social Sciences, Indian Institute of Technology Kharagpur, Kharagpur, India

This special issue foregrounds the region within diaspora studies through examining the representations of Punjab, a land-locked region divided between India and Pakistan after the partition of 1947. By bringing together papers that focus on plural imaginings of the region, the special issue throws light on the importance of the region rather than the nation for Punjabi diasporas. Through focusing on a number of Punjabi spaces and communities and engaging with Punjab as a geographical region, social construct and state of consciousness, the papers hope to contribute to broader debates on transnationalism, postnationalism, micronationalism and new identity narratives emerging in the twenty-first century.

The special issue's engagement with the region is framed within but also differs from transnational, Sikh and Punjab studies. Vertovec (1999, 1–2) described transnationalism

> as a condition in which, despite great distances and notwithstanding the presence of international borders (and all the laws, regulations and national narratives they represent), certain kinds of relationships have been globally intensified and now take place paradoxically in a planet-spanning yet common – however virtual – arena of activity.

Vertovec also suggested several themes – 'social morphology, as a type of consciousness, as a mode of cultural reproduction, as an avenue of capital, as a site of political engagement, and as a reconstruction of – "place" or locality' to disentangle the term (1999, 1). Punjabi diasporas, marginalized within the larger discourse of diaspora studies, have begun to receive due attention within the newly formed field of Sikh and Punjab studies that largely focuses on Sikh tradition (McLeod 1989; Singh and Barrier 1996; Grewal 1998) but has also directed academic attention to the region and the communities originating there (Dusenbury 1999; Gilmartin 2004; Talbot and Thandi 2004; Talbot 2007; Nesbitt 2011). In his essay 'The Diasporic Imaginary', Brian Keith Axel contested the 'place of origin' thesis dominating diaspora studies by arguing that 'for many diasporic groups, place, or place of origin, is not the primary issue' (2002, 411) citing the particular case of the Sikh diaspora and concluded that the 'imagined homeland' is the product of 'the diasporic imaginary' (Mishra 1996).

Axel's book *The Nation's Tortured Body: Violence, Representation, and the Formation of a Sikh Diaspora* (2001) that developed the idea further has radically altered the understanding of the relationship between the diaspora and the homeland. The idea of the homeland as a diasporic construct has been taken up in a number of essays that focus on the performance of Punjab through diasporic cultural practices (Baumann 1990; Bennett 2000; Dudrah 2002). However, Talbot (2007) has uncovered imperial acts of geographical and social reengineering that produced the region of Punjab that foreground construction as an intrinsic feature of the imagining of the Punjabi homeland. Similarly, Shackle (2014) has called attention to the repression of other languages such as Siraiki through their classification as dialects of Punjabi by the British to produce a unified Punjab and to the 'growing pressure for official recognition of Siraiki as a language distinct from Punjabi, and the consequent demand for the separation of the main Siraiki-speaking region from Punjab province'. Gilmartin (2004) interrogates the rural imaginary (Tatla 2004) charted on Punjab by asserting that both the Punjabi village and the Punjabi villager were colonial constructs.

Sensitive to these studies, this special issue focuses on the imagining of Punjab. In doing so, it deconstructs Punjab as an ethno-spatial but also as an ethno-linguistic and ethno-cultural construct produced through its imagining by the communities who dwell there, those who have left it and those formed by new narratives of the region. The idea behind the special issue was to move away from the originary myths of the region and identity that have dominated academic and mediatized representations of Punjab and to focus on the role of the imagination in producing Punjab. In particular, it hoped to reveal 'the rural imaginary' (Mooney 2011) to be a specifically Jat Sikh imaginary that has been historically mapped on Punjab through the production of Punjab as the granary of the British Empire during colonialism, a policy that was carried over in the post-colonial Indian state's rhetorical homage to the Punjabi farmer. This special issue aims to isolate imaginings of Punjab that are not centred on exclusivist regional, linguistic, sectarian or caste perspectives to propose the concept of *free-flowing cartographies* in relation to Punjab that facilitate its imaginings as a geographical region, a social construct and a state of consciousness. The region is imagined as a small place, a neighbourhood, a city, a village but also as performative traditions and everyday practices governing social relations and certain ways of doing things. While the essays engage with the particular region of Punjab, the ideas developed there have implications beyond Punjab. Thinking in terms of Punjab's free-flowing Punjabi cartographies underlines the constant crossing of boundaries between languages, cultures and sects in the Punjabi village (Oberoi 1994; Ahmed 2003; Ram 2008).

The papers in the special issue engage with plural imaginings of the region across several cities, nations, ethnic groups and genres. Through examining the fiction of two writers from Pakistan Punjab, Bapsi Sidhwa and Mohsin Hamid, Claire Chambers foregrounds their representation of Lahore, a province which had come to be equated with Punjab in the time of Akbar, as a post-colonial megacity that can be made to serve as a microcosm of Punjab and the nation. Arguing that Lahore is 'an unevenly developed, international urban centre, which constantly interpenetrates with and is cross-fertilized by its Punjabi rural hinterland', she points out that the representation of the interrelationship between heterogeneous groups of people in the two loci in the novels, the red light district of Heera Mandi and the nearby Badshahi mosque, enables exploration of metropolitan/hinterland dynamic in West Punjab. If Chambers foregrounds the diasporic imagining of Punjab through historically layered neighbourhoods of the 'Mughal City of Gardens', Kaveri Qureshi focuses on the deterritorialized 'Little Punjabs' of UK through tracing the established geographies of Punjabiness as illustrated by Thandi coach route maps and the significance of these interconnected hubs of Punjabiness for the emergence of belonging among second generation Punjabis. Through examining life history interviews of second generation Punjabis who grew up in provincial cities and towns off the Thandi coach route, she shows that they construct places like Southall Broadway and Soho Road as authentically Punjabi to demonstrate that such places can be crucibles of diasporic nostalgia and can 'decouple diaspora from originary homeland'. Virinder Kalra's essay contributes to the under-theorized idea of Punjabiat through exploring the biography and music of one of the most popular South Asian singers Nusrat Fateh Ali Khan. Through examining the relationship between non-essential Punjabiat and musical performativity, Kalra argues that the processes that 'operate to sustain musical and cultural continuity' tend to 'oscillate between the normatively demarcated zones of East Punjab, West Punjab and Punjabi diaspora'. In sharp contrast to Kalra who focuses on musical continuity to make a strong case for non-essential Punjabiat, Nukhbah Langah explores the poetry of two Siraiki poets, Khwaja Ghulam Farid and Riffat Abbas, to deconstruct the notion of an essentialized Punjabiat through their appropriation of the musical genre of Kafi. Through comparing the Kafis of the nineteenth century mystic poet with those of Abbas, she reveals Siraiki poets' appropriation of poetic and musical genres to resist colonial or Punjabi dominance and demonstrates how Abbas departs from the images and style of traditional Kafis of Farid to make a case for Siraiki difference. While Kalra cites linguistic and musical continuity to dissolve geographical boundaries, Langah reveals linguistic difference repressed in the construction of a generalized Punjabiat to strengthen claims for Siraiki separatism. Abbas Zaidi's essay brings another dimension to the linguistic debate through systematically investigating the paradoxical disappearance of Punjabi from West Punjab despite its Punjabi dominance. Through calling attention to the diasporization of Punjabi from Punjab, Zaidi disengages language from ethnic identity formation that has implications for the emergence of ethno-linguistic regionalisms. The final paper in the special issue brings a gendered perspective to bear upon the continuity of the Punjabi cultural precept of *izzat* in the diaspora through examining the biographies of two diasporic women, *Provoked* by Kiranjit Ahluwalia and Rahila Gupta; and *Shame* and *Daughters of Shame* by Jasvinder Sanghera. Through examining how the notion of *izzat* continues to regulate female behaviour even in diasporic families, Shweta Kushal and Evangeline Manickam reveal that resistance to Punjabi patriarchal structures is always contained through the recall of rural Punjabi norms.

The essays in the special issue bring a variety of disciplinary approaches to engage with the imagining of Punjab ranging from literary and cultural studies to sociology and sociolinguistics. They also draw on a wide range of methodologies, including literary and cultural analysis, ethnographic research (narratives and observation) and quantitative data analysis. There is clearly more room for research on the imagining of Punjab and that of other regions, communities and places of settlement. While most of the papers focused on the Pakistan Punjab and diasporic Punjab and literary and cultural texts produced there, there is ample scope for research that foregrounds its similarities for the Indian Punjab and other Punjabi communities. The essays in the special issue demonstrate the connections of Punjabi diaspora with the Punjab region that is imagined as a physical, social and mental construct rather than nation, language, religion or ethnicity, which has implications both for the importance of the imagining of the region within diaspora studies and the notion of the region itself as an imagined construct.

References

Ahmed, Ishtiaq. 2003. "Punjabis and Their Identity." *Daily Times Sunday*, February 23.

Axel, Brian Keith. 2001. *The Nation's Tortured Body: Violence, Representation, and the Formation of a Sikh Diaspora*. Durham: Duke University Press.

Axel, Brian Keith. 2002. "The Diasporic Imaginary." *Public Culture* 14 (2): 411–428.

Baumann, G. 1990. "The Re-Invention of Bhangra: Social Change and Aesthetic Shifts in a Punjabi Music in Britain." *World of Music* 32 (2): 81–95.

Bennett, A. 2000. *Popular Music and Youth Culture: Music, Identity and Place*. London: Macmillan.

Dudrah, Rajinder. 2002. "Cultural Production in the British Bhangra Music Industry: Music-Making, Locality, and Gender." *International Journal of Punjab Studies* 9: 219–251.

Dusenbury, Verne A. 1999. "Nation or World Religion? Master Narratives of Sikh Identity." In *Sikh Identity: Continuity and Change*, edited by Pashaura Singh and N. Gerald Barrier, 127–146. New Delhi: Manohar.

Gilmartin, David. 2004. "Migration and Modernity: The State, the Punjabi Village, and the Settling of the Canal Colonies." In *People on the Move: Punjabi Colonial, and Post-Colonial Migration*, edited by Ian Talbot and Shinder Thandi, 3–20. Karachi: Oxford University Press.

Grewal, J. S. 1998. *Contesting Interpretations of the Sikh Tradition*. New Delhi: Manohar.

McLeod, W. H. 1989. *The Sikhs: History, Religion, and Society*. New York: Columbia University Press.

Mishra, Vijay. 1996. "The Diasporic Imaginary: Theorizing the Indian Diaspora." *Textual Practice* 10 (3): 421–447.

Mooney, Nicola. 2011. *Rural Nostalgias and Transnational Dreams: Identity and Modernity Among Jat Sikhs*. Toronto: University of Toronto Press.

Nesbitt, E. 2011. "Sikh Diversity in the UK: Contexts and Evolution." In *Sikhs in Europe: Migration, Identities and Representations*, edited by K. A. Jacobsen and K. Myrvold, 225–252. Aldershot: Ashgate.

Oberoi, Harjot. 1994. The *Construction of Religious Boundaries: Culture, Identity, and Diversity in the Sikh Tradition*. Delhi: Oxford University Press.

Ram, Ronki. 2008. "Ravidass Deras and Social Protest: Making Sense of Dalit Consciousness in Punjab (India)." *Journal of Asian Studies* 67 (4): 1341–1364.

Shackle, Christopher. 2014. "Siraiki Language. Encyclopedia Britannica." Retrieved February 28, 2014. http://www.britannica.com/EBchecked/topic/535269/Siraiki-language

Singh, Pashaura and Gerald N. Barrier. 1996. *The Transmission of Sikh Heritage in the Diaspora*. New Delhi: Manohar.

Talbot, Ian. 2007. "Punjab Under Colonialism. The Punjab Under Colonialism: Order and Transformation in British India." *Journal of Punjab Studies* 14 (1): 3–10.

Talbot, Ian and Shinder Thandi, eds. 2004. *People on the Move: Punjabi Colonial, and Post-Colonial Migration*. Karachi: Oxford University Press.

Tatla, Darshan Singh. 2004. "The Rural Roots of the Sikh Diaspora." In *People on the Move: Punjabi Colonial, and Post-Colonial Migration*, edited by Ian Talbot and Shinder Thandi, 45–48. London: Oxford University Press.

Vertovec, Steven. 1999. "Conceiving and Researching Transnationalism." *Ethnic and Racial Studies* 22 (2): 447–462.

'The heart, stomach and backbone of Pakistan': Lahore in novels by Bapsi Sidhwa and Mohsin Hamid

Claire Chambers

Department of English and Related Literature, University of York, Heslington, York, UK

> Although much research has been undertaken on Indian cities, particularly Bombay/Mumbai, Calcutta/Kolkata and Delhi, Pakistani urban environments have not been subjected to anything like the same degree of scrutiny. There exists a long and rich history of artistic and textual interpretations of the city of Lahore, but this body of work has gone largely unappreciated in academic scholarship. To redress this critical gap, the article examines fiction by two diasporic authors from the Pakistani Punjab, Bapsi Sidhwa and Mohsin Hamid, for their representations of Lahore as a postcolonial megacity which is crucially important to the nation and the Punjab, and which interpenetrates with and is cross-fertilized by its Punjabi rural hinterland.

Introduction

In November 2013 an Indian television advertisement for Google entitled 'The Reunion' went viral on YouTube, garnering over four million hits from India, Pakistan and the wider world in just five days (Associated Press 2013; Google India 2013). The advert pivots on the friendship of two boys from different religious backgrounds who were separated due to the partition of the Indian subcontinent in 1947. Now an old man living in Delhi, the Hindu boy Baldev Mehra reminisces to granddaughter Saman about his younger years flying kites and stealing sweets in what is today's Pakistan. He recalls his best friend Yusuf especially fondly, and so, aided by the Google search engine and associated apps, Saman traces this fellow septugenarian and brings him to Delhi to be reunited with Baldev on the latter's birthday. The advertisement has generated largely positive reactions on both sides of the border, although Associated Press quotes one second-generation partition migrant's observation that it is not so easy for ordinary people to travel between India and Pakistan in the ongoing climate of hostility between the two countries (2013, n.p.)

However, for the purposes of this article about the city as a simultaneously material and textualized space, what is most noteworthy about 'The Reunion' is that Yusuf lives in Lahore, the antique city which Baldev and his family fled, never to return. Indeed, the way in which Lahore is represented in this tear-jerking commercial is indicative of the nostalgic diasporic lens through which the city is often depicted. Its opening scene features the call to prayer from a red-brick, white-domed mosque, which is presumably intended to be the city's most famous monument, the Badshahi Mosque, commissioned in the late seventeenth century by the Mughal emperor Aurangzeb (1618 – 1707). In the course of her research Saman googles Lahore's ancient history, parks, city gates and sweet shops – rich, culturally loaded and nostalgic images of the city. In this short film as in much other cultural production, Lahore is thus emblematic of partition and the shared history of these two hostile subcontinental neighbours. As Gyanendra Pandey puts it, partition's legacy is 'an extraordinary love – hate relationship' bifurcated between 'deep resentment and animosity, and the most militant of nationalism' and 'a considerable sense of nostalgia, frequently articulated in the view that this was a partition of siblings that should never have occurred' (2001, 2). The viral video tacitly supports and helps to answer this paper's central research questions: how are South Asian cities and regions imagined by their inhabitants, their diasporic communities and their artists? How does partition and its aftermath continue to impinge upon such imaginings of the Punjab, the province that was most affected by the violence and population exchange that occurred after partition?

This article stems from awareness that the Punjab has long been an area of key importance to pre-/colonial India and to postcolonial India and Pakistan. The two Punjabs experienced overlapping but distinct residues of British imperialism, great trauma in partition, relative economic vitality and hegemony within their nations, and centrality in the reinventions and imaginings of the postcolonial Indian and Pakistani nation-states. In an effort to enhance understandings of Punjabi literature, history and anthropology, I examine depictions of the Pakistani Punjab, and particularly its ancient capital of Lahore, in texts by Bapsi Sidhwa and Mohsin Hamid, two important writers who are from that city and are among its most observant chroniclers. However, given this article's location in *South Asian Diaspora*, I have chosen these writers in part because they have spent significant proportions of their lives in the diaspora, specifically the USA. Their perspectives on the city are therefore to some extent shaped by what Walder (2011) terms 'postcolonial nostalgia'.[1] Sidhwa (born 1938) is from the generation affected by India's partition and the creation of Pakistan, while Hamid was born in 1971, the year of a second partition after a bloody civil war which resulted in Bangladesh seceding from the Pakistani union. As well as exploring their representations of the city's topographical, cultural, religious and linguistic diversity, the essay also examines a central locus of Lahore as depicted in the novels: the iconic red light district, Heera Mandi, which stands incongruously close to the religious site the Badshahi Mosque.

Much research from various disciplines has been conducted in relation to Indian cities, particularly Bombay/Mumbai (see, for example, Hansen 2001; Mehta 2005; Patel and Thorner 1995; Prakash 2010), Calcutta/Kolkata (Chaudhuri 1990, 1995; Dutta 2008; Gupta, Mukherjee, and Banerjee 2009) and, to a somewhat lesser extent, Delhi (Dalrymple 1994; Hosagrahar 2005; Kaul 1997). However, Pakistani urban environments have been strikingly underrepresented, with Karachi and especially Lahore receiving a small amount of scholarly attention in comparison with the vast archive on Bombay.[2] In an attempt to fill this lacuna, I examine Sidhwa's work, especially her acclaimed partition novel *Cracking India* (1991), alongside Mohsin Hamid's three novels, for their textualized descriptions of Lahore as a postcolonial city and as the heart of the Punjab and of Pakistan more broadly. I then weave in the theoretical approaches of Fredric Jameson, Edward W. Soja, Michel Foucault,

Michel de Certeau and others, which allow the same geographical locations to be framed as a dynamic space of social and cultural contestations.

But what is it about Lahore that has apparently made it invisible to literary and other humanities scholars, while other South Asian cities, such as Delhi, Calcutta and Mumbai, have been vociferously celebrated by critics? The first reason for this neglect is that Lahore is in Pakistan, a country with a troubled and variable relationship with the West, and with its own internal problems apropos of scholarship. Ever since Zia-ul-Haq's regime, which was bankrolled by the USA as part of Cold War strategy, censorship has been institutionalized at the heart of Pakistani governance. While the media opened up dramatically during Pervez Musharraf's military rule (1999–2008), Pakistani higher education institutions, particularly their arts departments, still chafe under restrictions and a lack of funding which hobble indigenous research. Second, Lahore used to be an important destination along the hippie trail (loosely mapped onto the old Silk Route), but after the Iranian Revolution of 1979 and occupations of Afghanistan by the USSR and later the USA, ordinary tourists could no longer enter or exit Pakistan's western gateways with ease, meaning that fewer outsiders have had a chance to be inspired by the city's history and culture in the way that Indian cities have spawned their Mark Tullys, William Dalrymples and Dominique Lapierres. Finally, in relation to urban studies, it is Karachi that grabs the headlines, in part because its megacity status dwarfs Lahore's, with populations of approximately 9.4 and 5.2 million, respectively. Karachi's higher profile is also due to its disproportionately larger population of *muhajirs* (the migrants and descendants of migrants who fled from India to Pakistan during and after partition) and attendant ethnic and political conflict, which attracts much scholarly attention (see, for example, Anjaria and McFarlane 2011, 298–337).

Yet Lahore could not matter more in terms of its history and hold on the South Asian imagination; its location and strategic importance as a hub connecting India and Khyber Pakthunkhwa, formerly known as the Northwest Frontier Province; and its economic productivity in the manufacturing and communications industries. As I show in this essay, the city's close proximity to the almost impregnable Wagah border means that it is uniquely vulnerable when the two nations of India and Pakistan square up to each other, as they do periodically, for example in the nuclear standoff of late 1990s and the crisis following the Indian parliament attacks of 2001.[3] More positively, Lahore is the cultural capital of Pakistan, even if it has never been the political or administrative capital of anything larger than the Punjab province. In 1940, it was in the city's Iqbal Park that Jinnah issued what became known as the Lahore Resolution, advocating the creation of Pakistan through an inchoate plan for 'autonomous national States' within independent India that would allegedly 'allow the major nations separate homelands' (Jinnah 1994, 55). Lahore has long been Pakistan's social and cultural heartland; its landmarks provide architectural testament to the many pasts which have overlaid the city, making it a palimpsest and the space of intersecting identities, many of which pre-date colonial India by centuries if not millennia. The metropolis has a vibrant arts scene that is diminished because of partition but is still clearly present, and I discuss the work and reception of one of its visual artists Iqbal Hussain in the next section. Lahore also matters because it acts a barometer of the changes that are happening in Pakistan. Unlike Karachi with its high numbers of *muhajirs* and ethnic violence, Lahore has until recently been a relatively peaceful city. However, the last five years have witnessed a sea change in relation to terror, sectarian violence and international machinations. I argue that Sidhwa and Hamid trace the genesis of this transformation back to the class, gender and ethnic divisions that have always been present in the city and which were exacerbated by the creation of Pakistan.

A personal view

This section is structured around my own impressions of and anecdotes about Lahore; these are underpinned by research and by recognition that scholarship is never wholly disinterested, culturally neutral and allowing access to objective 'truth'. Soon after my arrival in Lahore in 2011 for my first visit in nearly two decades (I went back for two further sojourns in the subsequent years), the friend I was staying with took me to Faiz Ghar, the former home of Faiz Ahmed Faiz (1911–1984). Faiz was associated with the leftist Progressive Writers Association and was widely considered one of Pakistan's finest poets. His poems were made into songs, sung by well-known singers like Noor Jehan and Tina Sani, so they are famous throughout Pakistan and its diaspora. Faiz Ghar is now an art gallery, which is run by Faiz's daughter, the feminist, activist, painter and art critic Salima Hashmi. At this house of the arts and liberal education, Hashmi shook my hand, declaring in an impish tone, 'Welcome to the Land of the Pure'. However, in the aftermath of the assassination of Hashmi's first cousin, the Punjab governor, Salman Taseer, for allegedly calling Pakistan's corruption-ridden blasphemy legislation a 'black law', during that trip I was to discover that the chasm between 'impure', outspoken liberals and those known locally as *fundos* or fundamentalists is growing increasingly wide.

While I witnessed elite groups of artists, academics and other professionals discussing politics and poetry with similar passion over copious amounts of illegal alcohol, it was sobering to watch as every vehicle entering university campuses was searched with under-car mirrors to check for bombs. Lahore is still coming to terms with its new status as a target for terrorists, made especially apparent in the gun attack on the Sri Lankan cricket team there in 2009, lethal bombs detonated in the Sufi shrine Data Darbar in 2010, and the case of a 'diplomat' Ray Davis (later revealed to be a CIA contractor) who fatally shot two men and killed another in a hit and run accident on 27 January 2011. Yet despite the 'blowback' from this last incident and from unmanned drone killings by the USA which is encapsulated in the rise of the Pakistani Taliban, there is another Lahore, that of Faiz and his daughter, cultural and intellectual energy, pluralism, tolerance, the arts and sexuality. Yet it should go without saying that Lahore is not a space – as represented in fiction, life writing or scholarship – that can or should be mapped in terms of binaries. If my recent trips and research have shown me one thing, it is the absence of uniformity in Pakistan and the city which is arguably its most accurate microcosm, Lahore.

To anyone who disagrees with the idea that Lahore is representative of Pakistan more broadly, it is worth thinking of Anatol Lieven, who, in a section of his book *Pakistan: A Hard Country* entitled 'Lahore, the Historic Capital', mistakenly writes: 'Pakistan is the heart, stomach and backbone of Pakistan. Indeed, in the view of many of its inhabitants, it *is* Pakistan' (Lieven 2011, 267). This tautological but revealing substitution of 'Pakistan' for 'Lahore' chimes with the saying Lahoris use, almost shruggingly, to emphasize their city's distinctiveness: *Lahore, Lahore aye* (Lahore is Lahore). The northeastern city is the cultural heartland of the country, with a detailed recorded history going back to the tenth century CE, and a much longer oral, cultural and communitarian presence. Its economic powerhouse status and the hold it has on the Pakistani imagination, particularly through the movies of Lollywood (the nation's film industry, based in Lahore), have also meant large-scale migration from the rural areas to Punjab's capital in order to find work.

From the dire situation of many women in Lahore (which I will explore in the later textual analysis), to the intelligence, independence, and creative power of Salima Hashmi and others, the picture revealed is extremely complex. Lahore is often seen as a pleasure city,[4] and Mohsin Hamid in particular is interested in millennial Pakistan's voluptuary, ecstasy-taking social whirl, as well as more familiar scenes of violence and stark class divisions. His debut novel *Moth Smoke* (2000) was viewed by Anita Desai as a turning point for subcontinental literature, in that it was one of the earliest twenty-first-century novels to depart from the Indian magic realism fashionable in the 1980s and 1990s and venture into darker and generically indeterminate territory inspired by his hometown Lahore (Desai 2000, n.p.). Indeed, for many, the metropolis represents pain, exploitation and danger. Or, as Sidhwa (2005) puts it in her anthology on Lahore, this is at once a city of sin and splendour. Even the Lahore of the late 1970s and early 1980s under the viciously Islamizing Zia ul-Haq regime is portrayed in Sidhwa's novel fourth novel *An American Brat* as a city of 'paradoxes, where bold women of a certain class often wield as much clout as pistol-toting thugs' (1994, 192). To enrich Desai's analysis of *Moth Smoke* as a seminal text within an emerging renaissance of Pakistani fiction, therefore, we might locate it within an alternative canon of writing on the Punjab, or what is often termed the *Punjabiyat* (linguistic nation of the Punjab), from Anglo-Indian writers such as Flora Annie Steel and Rudyard Kipling, to such evocative storytellers of partition as Amrita Pritam and adopted Lahori Saadat Hasan Manto, to the more recent Khushwant Singh and Bapsi Sidhwa, and now such diasporic writers as Daljit Nagra, Amarjit Chandan, Daniyal Mueenuddin and Tariq Ali.

My second, even shorter anecdote concerns artist Iqbal Hussain (Figure 1), who runs Cooco's Den (Figure 2), a restaurant in Lahore's famous red light district of Heera Mandi, which ironically stands in the shadow of Pakistan's most famous mosque, the beautiful Badshahi Masjid. Hussain set up Cooco's Den to support his mother and sister who are both prostitutes from the *Kanjari* caste who carry out sex work and music in the historic area of Heera Mandi or the Market of Diamonds (the more cynical, like Prince Kamaruddin in Sidhwa's debut novel *The Crow Eaters* ([1980] 1982), suggest that it is more accurately described as a flesh market: 'Plenty of gems – walking around on two legs!' ([1980] 1982, 131)). Hussain is also an acclaimed artist, who exhibits his paintings of sex workers (Figure 3) on the walls of Cooco's Den, as well as displaying statues of nudes, Hindu gods and so on. This unorthodox, bohemian restauranteur has been on the receiving end of threats and antagonism from the Islamic Right, because to them he represents godlessness and/or creeping Hinduization, female sexuality and general transgression. However, Hussain considers it his duty to paint the lives of the matrilineal dancing girl community from which he comes. In her book *The State of Islam*, Saadia Toor writes, 'the artist was not allowed to exhibit his work at the state-run Alhamra Art Gallery in Lahore because they were deemed "obscene". In protest, Hussain exhibited them on the roadside near the gallery' (2011, 151).

Notwithstanding the whiff of scandal surrounding them, Heera Mandi and Cooco's Den restaurant are increasingly becoming the trendy playground of the rich, liberal and not so liberal classes who are happy to pay European prices for cappuccinos and curries overlooking the Badshahi Mosque. As Louise Brown remarks, 'There's something exciting and illicit about coming here, something that makes respectable Pakistani

Figure 1. Iqbal Hussain (© for all three photographs: Claire Chambers).

pulses race' (2006, 8). Once again we have paradoxes: between the urban, urbane upper-middle-class flâneur and the vulnerable street-walker; between the arts and sexuality on the one hand, and austere Deobandi Muslim conservatism on the other. In her book *Heera Mandi* Claudine Le Tournier d'Ison and her translator express this diversity in non-politically correct language:

> The street resembled a court of miracles – handicapped beggars, cripples rolling in a ball on the ground, tramps in the last shreds of a shalwar kameez, and emaciated drug addicts [...] within [the] misshapen walls looked like a junkyard for all of society's most depraved – dealers, prostitutes, pimps and of course, Shi'as, as rejected as the Christians. The only ones who dared enter here were the bourgeois in need of excitement, ready to mix with the riff-raff at the cost of their virtue, politicians who by day proudly brandished the Quran, and by night the bank notes that they showered on the dancers. (2012, 88–89)

Here, Le Tournier d'Ison recognizes the almost carnivalesque intermixture in Heera Mandi of those usually considered society's dregs – sex workers and their keepers, drug users and their suppliers, many of them Shi'a (a sect increasingly despised in frantically Sunni-izing Pakistan) – alongside those at the top of the social pile: patriarchs, politicians and the pious.

Tracery of urbanization

Lahore is an unevenly developed, international urban centre, which productively intersects with and is cross-fertilized by the well-irrigated rural hinterland in this 'Land of

Figure 2. Cooco's Den.

Five Rivers', so that the city is not easily separable from its outlying countryside. On first glance, my last statement might seem to be contradicted by Hamid's third and most recent novel *How to Get Filthy Rich in Rising Asia*, in which the text's protagonist, 'you', comes from an archetypal Punjabi village, in which workers genuflect to *zamindars* or feudal landlords, women carry pots on their head, and water buffalo are milked while they chew on fodder (2013, 8–9). Yet this is by no means an idealized rural setting: when the main character's father surveys it, far from noticing the deliberately clichéd pastoral tropes, he instead sees 'the labor by which a farmer exchanges his allocation of time in this world for an allocation of time in this world. Here, in the heady bouquet of nature's pantry, your father sniffs mortality' (2013, 7–8). For these reasons of hardship and mortality, most of the novel's rural dwellers long, in the words of the opening chapter's title, to 'Move to the City', where they know wages to be high but do not realize that expenses are equally lofty. The protagonist migrates to a city which it becomes clear is Lahore (although places and people are unnamed in this novel, perhaps to lend it a universality that accords with its ironic structuring as a self-help book). During his relocation to the metropolis, the focalizer witnesses:

> a passage of time that outstrips its chronological equivalent. Just as when headed into the mountains a quick shift in altitude can vault one from subtropical jungle to semi-arctic tundra, so too can a few hours on a bus from rural remoteness to urban centrality appear to span millennia. (2013, 14)

This passage suggests that even though there is only a relatively short physical distance between the forelock-tugging, pitcher-carrying, buffalo-milking villagers and the city

Figure 3. Iqbal Hussain's art.

of pollution, dual carriageways, electricity and advertising hoardings, culturally they are as dissimilar as jungle and tundra. It perhaps echoes Salman Rushdie's notion in *The Satanic Verses* that his Indian-born characters Saladin and Gibreel do not fly very far, despite crossing the more than five thousand miles between Bombay and London, 'because they rose from one great city, fell to another. The distance between cities is always small; a villager, travelling a hundred miles to town, traverses emptier, darker, more terrifying space' (Rushdie 1988, 41). Later on in Hamid's novel, the protagonist similarly reflects on the 'yawning gap between countryside and city' (2013, 146).

Despite this first impression of the book, in an interview with me, Hamid complicates such a bifurcatory picture of urban and rural Punjab:

> I think the rural/urban split is blurring, because all along Pakistan's many major roads, there's an urbanization taking place. If you drive around the GT Road, or any other large road in Punjab, little towns and shops have grown up around it. People live along those roads, have electricity, televisions, satellite dishes, and mobile phone coverage, and they watch the cars passing through. They are traders, selling things in their shops, and paying for services. They are not like the farmers. This network cuts across all of Punjab now, so it isn't as though there's an urban core and then periphery, but a tracery of urbanization that penetrates the periphery. (Chambers 2011, 182–183)

Such a sketch is filled out in *How to Get Filthy Rich in Rising Asia* when 'the region that forms the economic hinterland to your metropolis' is described:

The car approaches the outskirts of the city, passing the disinterred earth and linear mounds of vast middle-class housing developments. Rows of electricity poles rise in various stages of completion, some bare, some bridged by taut cables, occasionally one from which wires dangle to the ground. (2013, 88–89)

This portrayal of Lahore's outskirts dramatizes the 'tracery of urbanization' which Hamid sketched in the interview. His description of the exposed soil and incomplete electricity pylons suggests that here we see an unfinished, in-between space that is neither urban nor rural, but fuzzy. This interstitial area of the suburbs is seen as having neither the danger and promise of the city, nor the bucolic idyll and grinding poverty of the country but, as rents and demand for urban space soar ever higher, urbanization is encroaching on the suburbs too. Cropland in the outer suburbs is increasingly being sold off to developers (2013, 90; 165; 219) and the narrator acknowledges the porous nature of the city's borderlines: '[y]our city is not laid out as a single-celled organism with a wealthy nucleus surrounded by an ooze of slums. [...] Accordingly, the poor live near the rich' (Hamid 2013, 22). To some extent, then, Hamid recognizes with Ian Talbot that 'Punjabi society [is] overwhelmingly rural' and that '[t]raditional rural customs and values lay just beneath the veneer of urban sophistication and culture' (Talbot 1988, 13; 15).

Similarly, in Hamid's debut novel *Moth Smoke*, we are told that Dilaram, now the madam of a brothel in Heera Mandi, was propelled to the city when, as a young village girl from rural Punjab, she had been repeatedly raped by her landlord and his relatives, and later sent into bonded prostitution in Lahore (2000, 50–51). Some doubt is cast over this story, however, as the protagonist Daru thinks she seems 'a little too well spoken for an uneducated village girl, sounding more like a wayward Kinnaird alumna to me' (2000, 51). Whether Dilaram really was an innocent peasant girl who got caught up in human trafficking and prostitution, akin to Douloti in Mahasweta Devi's story 'Douloti the Bountiful' (1995), or she is in fact a sophisticated urbanite who attended a prestigious school like Lahore's Kinnaird College for Women, is never resolved in the narrative.

La Whore: gendering the city

Nonetheless, this moment from *Moth Smoke* establishes Heera Mandi as a space in which young girls from the country and city put their bodies on display, evade the cops, and are exploited by predatory pimps. Even more extensively, in *Cracking India* Sidhwa paints a vivid picture of Heera Mandi as a place where poetry and music flourishes. The area was originally built as a sanctuary for the illegitimate sons of Moghul emperors and their *tawaifs*, also known as nautch-girls or courtesans, who during the Raj era at least were mostly Muslim women from North India. The exploitation of women, many of them from the countryside, went hand in hand with an attempt to dress this up in glamorous ways. Although *ghazals*, often composed, recited and sung in red light districts such as Heera Mandi, are also a typically Muslim poetic form, the association with courts, courtesans and dancing girls to some extent caused them to contain recurring, apparently un-Islamic images such as the nightingale, wine, roses and the beloved, although these metaphors also reflect the Sufi devotee's longing for God (Matthews, Shackle, and Husain 2003, 32–37). Sidhwa's villain Ice-candy-man uses the elevated language of *ghazals* in order to shower the kidnapped Hindu Ayah with praise, particularly ironically in the following instance, as it is he that has forced her into the dancing-girl profession he extols here:

> She lives to dance! And I to toast her dancer's grace!
> Princes pledge their lives to celebrate her celebrated face! (1991, 259)

However, despite his most poetic efforts, his exploitation of Ayah is evident in her diminished figure and downcast glance: as feminists often point out, the flip-side of idealization is abuse.

As these examples suggest, Heera Mandi is a central locus of Lahore's Walled City, vividly depicted in novels by Sidhwa and Hamid. The red light district is very near the Minar-e-Pakistan, a tower built in the 1960s to commemorate the 1940 Lahore Resolution, and adjacent to Lahore's most famous landmark, the enormous Mughal mosque, Badshahi Masjid. Other nearby Mughal sites include Anarkali Bazaar, Shalimar Gardens and Jehangir's Mausoleum. By highlighting the diversity and history of this district, I want to suggest that Heera Mandi can be read a microcosm of the city as a whole, and therefore of the Punjab more broadly, just as Lahore may in some ways be read as the nation in miniature. Yet, unsurprisingly, few in Pakistan are willing to recognize the 'female street' (Sidhwa [1983] 2008, 60) of Heera Mandi as a touchstone for the Fatherland, as Fouzia Saeed indicates:

> Identified by various names, it represents one of the oldest flesh markets in the land, where prostitution and the performing arts are linked in a complex web of human relations. Hardly any informed citizen can plead ignorance of the residents of this area, but they are considered the least entitled to be understood by their fellow beings. (Saeed 2002, vii)

In the red light district binaries are broken down, given the contiguity of the nearby Badshahi Mosque and also given the professed religiosity of many of the area's Shi'a sex workers. Naheem Jabbar observes that '[t]he self-conscious piety of the women [in the red light district Heera Mandi] contradicts the ideas that they are so generically typical of profanity (woman *qua* profanity)' (2011, 109). The authors' representations of the heterogeneous nature of the people who congregate in the two very different areas of red light district and mosque allow them to explore the metropole/hinterland dynamic. References to the mosque also necessitate discussion of the important and changing role of religion – the majority faith Islam and, to a lesser extent, the minority creed of Zoroastrianism to which Sidhwa and the Parsi community belong – in contributing towards post-partition Lahori identity. In an elegiac section of *An American Brat*, Sidhwa reflects on the increasing religification not only of Muslims in Pakistan, but of the formerly tolerant Parsis community:

> These established custodians of the Zoroastrian doctrine were no less rigid and ignorant than the fundos in Pakistan. This mindless current of fundamentalism sweeping the world like a plague had spared no religion, not even their microscopic community of 120 thousand. (1994, 305–306)

It is useful to keep this even-handed reminder in mind, rather than accepting the widespread contemporary assumption that the rise of religious sentiment is limited to Muslims and mosques.

A sexualization of the city (La Whore) is perhaps best articulated in *The Pakistani Bride* ([1983] 2008):

> Lahore – the ancient whore, the handmaiden of dimly remembered Hindu kings, the courtesan of Moghul Emperors, bedecked and bejeweled, savaged by marauding hordes. Healed by the caressing hands of successive lovers. A little shoddy ... like an attractive but ageing concubine, ready to bestow surprising delights on those who cared to court her – proudly displaying Royal gifts. (2008, 43)

Here, Sidhwa alludes to the 'succeeding lovers' who have conquered Lahore, from the pre-Mughal 'Hindu kings' to the 'Mughal emperors', and implicitly from the Shivaji and Durrani Empires, the Sikh leader Ranjit Singh, and the British colonizers to the postcolonial Pakistani politicians who have ruled Lahore and West Punjab. Personifying the city as a fading but still attractive, somewhat tawdry figure, she evokes Lahore's loss of its multicultural identity after partition, which is also reflected in *Cracking India*: 'The garden scene has depressingly altered. Muslim families who added color when scattered among the Hindus and Sikhs, now monopolize the garden, depriving it of color' (1991, 249). Elsewhere in *The Pakistani Bride*, there is a sustained passage about Heera Mandi (2008, 57–65), which contains strikingly similar motifs to those found in her first novel, *The Crow Eaters* ([1980] 1982, 130–138). Both depict men chewing betel leaves and proffering money; women in gaudy dress (*churidar* pyjamas, ankle-bells and heavy makeup) going through the movements of dance in a 'mechanical' fashion while accompanied by harmonium, sitar and tabla; and Heera Mandi's narrow streets, decrepit wooden buildings, trellises and balconies. The recurring characters of a middle-aged madam, young girls of varying degrees of fairness, plumpness and innocence, and sinister pimps in each text suggest that many features of Heera Mandi *qua* space have changed little in the last 100 years.

Space in theory and the imagination

But what constitutes space? Since the mid-1970s a theoretical perspective has emerged that Western accounts of history are incomplete, due to an excessive concentration on the temporal perspective, at the expense of the spatial dimension. Michel Foucault famously indicts Western thought as a whole for its inattention to geography: 'Space was treated as the dead, the fixed, the undialectical, the immobile. Time, on the contrary, was richness, fecundity, life, dialectic' (1980, 70). He identifies a dichotomy of thinking about time and space, suggesting that since the nineteenth century space has largely been ignored by philosophers, while time and history have been accorded great attention. His calls for greater attention to space led to what many have summarized as the 'spatial turn' in the social sciences and humanities (Raju 2011, 1; Teverson and Upstone 2011, ix). This turn towards geography specifically from within postcolonial studies is exemplified by such texts as Mary Louise Pratt's *Imperial Eyes* (1992), James Holston and Arjun Appadurai's *Cities and Citizenship* (1999), Gyan Prakash's (2010) *Mumbai Fables* and Andrew Teverson and Sara Upstone's *Postcolonial Spaces* (2011). I concentrate on one thinker in particular, Edward W. Soja, because his ideas from *Postmodern Geographies* (1989) that space has three manifestations is helpful in thinking about Lahore, and I would argue that it is borne out in the novels. Soja makes a tripartite distinction between 'space *per se*, space as a contextual given, and socially-based spatiality' (1989, 79). He is interested in the way in which space is primordially given, yet is also an effect of social production and imaginative construction.

First, Soja argues that in commonsense perspective space is a given, relatively unchanging physical reality that has a profound effect on its inhabitants. This is demonstrated in Lahore's status as a frontier city, just 30 miles away from hostile Indian territory, which means it would likely be the first place of attack in any nuclear war between the two countries. Hamid is especially alert to the impact this has on the city's residents, and in *Moth Smoke* 'if they nuke Lahore' is a frequent refrain (2000, 88, 91, 92). Other sorts of violence in the city also have a levelling effect on Lahore's residents, whether rich or poor, shaping their behaviour and fears and limiting their movements. After his mother is killed by a stray bullet (perhaps from a wedding celebration) while asleep on a charpoy on the roof during a baking Punjabi summer, Daru has a recurring dream in which he 'imagine[s] Lahore as a city with bullets streaking into the air' (Hamid 2000, 108). This prefigures the later standoff between Pakistan and India over nuclear tests, which is especially tensely felt in Lahore, the municipality on the frontline between the two:

> The entire city is uneasy. Sometimes, when monsoon lightning slips a bright explosion under the clouds, there is a pause in conversations. Teacups halt, steaming, in front of extended lips. Lightning's echo comes as thunder. And the city waits for thunder's echo, for a wall of heat that burns Lahore with the energy of a thousand summers, a million partitions, a billion atomic souls split in half. (Hamid 2000, 211)

An examination of the language usage here reveals the exaggeration of 'entire city' and the sense of tension and waiting followed by the nuclear sunburst of fire and light. This is reminiscent, you notice, not just of the nuclear holocausts of Hiroshima and Nagasaki, but of Lahore's own holocaust of partition, which is explicitly referenced in the passage. Clearly even space that appears to be a stable, de facto entity is actually socially constructed and, although it is more likely to cause problems for the poor, it can be also be turned against the tea-sipping middle classes, engulfing them in violence and terror.

Therefore, according to Soja, the second understanding of urban space is as a socially manipulated, changeable material that is produced as much as it produces and involves 'social translation, transformation, and experience' (1989, 79–80). Both Soja and his theoretical forerunner Henri Lefebvre ([1974], 1991) write compelling accounts of the ways in which city planning is intimately related to ideology and methods of social control. Yet both theorists recognize that the attempts of the powerful to monopolize the social production of space are never entirely successful. The intentions of town planners are modified or subverted by the uses locals make of their space 'on the ground' and city dwellers have varying degrees of agency to transform their surroundings.

We need only look at the depiction of Lahore's Lawrence Gardens (now the Bagh-e-Jinnah) and other locations in Sidhwa's *Cracking India* to see that space can be radically re-constructed by its residents. The nanny character, Ayah, who is in many ways a gendered personification of independent India (*Bharat Mata* or Mother India), meets her admirers in Lawrence Gardens on the Upper Mall near Charing Cross. Her beauty at first unites members of many different religious groups, so that they sit together in relative harmony, discussing current events and gossip under a Raj-era monument. In contrast to this statue of Queen Victoria, which is 'cast in gunmetal, [...] majestic, overpowering, ugly', Ayah is described as resembling 'the Hindu goddess she worships'

(Sidhwa 1991, 28, 12), and everything about her is depicted as soft, attractive, and fertile. Ayah is an allegorical representation of the youthful promise of Indian Independence in comparison with the austere decay of the old British order, and in the park she subverts the colonial space around her. But later, when the group stops meeting under the symbol of the British Raj and instead starts to meet at an Indian restaurant, the group's unity disintegrates, suggesting that existing tensions between different groups are exacerbated once the common enemy has departed. As the accord between Ayah's courtiers breaks down and a more vicious struggle begins for her approval (and, by implication, for control over her body), it becomes evident that the city is splintering along ethnic lines and the different religious groups are making it impossible for each other to meet within the same spaces.

The third way in which Soja argues that we experience space is through its construction in the imagination. This is what Fredric Jameson terms 'cognitive mapping' (1984, 89), through which term he shows that we all have our own mental maps of the cities in which we live. Jameson emphasizes the social, collective nature of this mental cartography, suggesting that each of us positions our subjective consciousness within 'unlived, abstract conceptions of the geographic totality' (1984, 90), which may however be 'garbled' or distorted reflections of cultural biases (1988, 353). The concept serves as a reminder that space is as much created by the imagination as by civic leaders and planners. William Glover, the preeminent scholar of Lahore as urban space, concurs, writing, 'Any city is created as much imaginatively as it is physically of bricks and mortar' (2011, xv), while Anatol Lieven makes this more specific when he writes: 'Lahore is a city of the imagination, in a way that bureaucratic Islamabad and dour, impoverished Peshawar cannot be, and Karachi has not yet had the time to become (though writers like Kamila Shamsie are working on it)' (Lieven 2011, 268).

It could be said that cities in South Asia, especially those with history as ancient as Lahore's, are so layered with sets of different pasts, that they form distinct 'chronotopes' (a fictional construction of time–space; the term is from Bakhtin 2004). Thus Lucknow, Lahore and Delhi, associated as they were and continue to be with an Islamic past of high culture, occupy a particular terrain in the subcontinent's symbolic and imaginary realms (Lacan [1981] 1998, 279–280). My thinking on this aspect of the space is particularly informed by the following comment by Michel Foucault:

> The mirror is, after all, a utopia, since it is a placeless place. In the mirror, I see myself there where I am not, in an unreal, virtual space that opens up behind the surface; I am over there, there where I am not, a sort of shadow that gives my own visibility to myself, that enables me to see myself there where I am absent: such is the utopia of the mirror. But it is also a heterotopia in so far as the mirror does exist in reality, where it exerts a sort of counteraction on the position that I occupy. (1986, 24)

Here, Foucault alerts us to the fact that the flat, limited object of the mirror creates a vast, three-dimensional space beyond its frame. He terms this a heterotopia, meaning a liminal space situated somewhere between the real and the utopian space of the imagination, a composite space which juxtaposes several spaces within one site. Heterotopic space is 'placeless' and 'virtual', but Foucault argues that it is worthy of the same level of theoretical attention as geographical spaces. It is a space which can only be travelled in the imagination; this 'through the looking-glass' world is almost the same as our own, but exists as an inverted version. As Foucault puts it, heterotopias are 'a kind of effectively enacted utopia in which the real sites, all other real sites that can be found within the culture, are simultaneously represented, contested, and inverted' (Foucault 1986, 24). Other examples Foucault gives of these 'in-between spaces' include the cemetery, the cinema, and such 'heterotopias of deviation' as psychiatric hospitals, prisons and old people's homes, to which we could add the brothel of Heera Mandi, or Lahore more broadly. These spaces at once function as 'real places' and as utopian/dystopian localities on which to project the culture's fears and desires.

Furthermore, as Foucault recognizes, the 'virtual space' created by the mirror has a destabilizing and yet reconstituting effect on the identity. Foucault's repetition of the phrase 'there where I am not' (*là où je ne suis pas*) articulates the paradox of the mirror, which projects an image of the self onto a place that does not exist. Foucault describes the mirror image of the self as a 'shadow', an insubstantial being displaced from its 'real' location. Yet the shadowy nature of the mirror image is offset by the way in which Foucault argues that it also acts as a 'counteraction on the position that I occupy'. When we look in a mirror Foucault suggests that we imagine ourselves to be the 'mirror person'; we look back at ourselves from this disembodied perspective and begin to reconstruct our identity from an outsider's point of view.

This depiction of the mirror allowing the conceptualization of a whole, unbroken identity of course contains parallels with Lacan's notion of the Mirror Stage, to which I alluded earlier. Lacan uses the Mirror Stage to symbolize the moment in a child's life when it sees its own reflection and realizes that it is separate from its mother. At this point, the child leaves the Imaginary world, associated with the mother's body, a composite identity, and incoherent babbling, and enters the Real or Symbolic realm, where 'the Rule of the Father' is paramount, identity becomes fixed and complete, and language is acquired. I do not wish to elaborate on Lacan's complex and much disputed theory in greater detail.[5] What I want to emphasize instead is the way in which the Mirror Stage marks 'the genesis of bodily boundaries' (Butler 1993, 71); in other words, it encourages the realization that one's identity is unique and differentiated from other people's. Just as geographical boundaries signify proximity to one's neighbours while at the same time emphasizing difference, so too the heterotopic boundary of the mirror projects a similar image onto the other side of a dividing line. This is important because of Lahore's closeness to the border with India and the impact that partition has had on the city's collective imagination. Some would say that the Lucknowis who ended up in Lahore feel it is not the centre of culture that Lucknow was, and others who left Lahore and ended up in Lucknow or Delhi have a mirrored sense of nostalgia for their own abandoned city. Amitav Ghosh, in his novel *The Shadow Lines* describes Calcutta as standing along a 'looking-glass border' facing its inverted twin Dhaka ([1988] 2008, 257). Additionally, people who have spent much time in the diaspora (the USA for both Hamid and Sidhwa, with Hamid having spent an additional seven years working in London) also construct an identity for the city, and by extension themselves, which is often distorted through the convex mirror of spatial and temporal distance. As such, there is much nostalgia and even a sense of loss with which the city is associated in public memory.

A disjuncture between this city of the imagination and the metropolitan world of everyday lived materialism discussed earlier is illustrated in Hamid's second novel, *The Reluctant Fundamentalist* (2007), in which the protagonist, Changez, muses on the city's Mughal history and historic textures to a sceptical and materialist American businessman:

> I said I was from Lahore, the second largest city of Pakistan, ancient capital of the Punjab, home to nearly as many people as New York, layered like a sedimentary plain with the

accreted history of invaders from the Aryans to the Mongols to the British. He merely nodded. Then he said, 'And are you on financial aid?' (Hamid 2007, 7)

It is worth noting that William Glover's research accords with Changez's imaginative view, expressed here, that Lahore is a palimpsest in which British architecture is grafted onto layers of pre-Mughal, Mughal and Sikh history. According to Glover, there is a surprising amount of interchange between Lahore's bustling Old City and the apparently spatially quarantined Raj-era civil station. For example, from the year of the Indian Uprising (1857) until 1891, St James's Church found itself formally consecrated and housed in Anarkali's Tomb, the last resting place of a Muslim dancing girl (2007, 19). This woman, Anarkali, is said to have been the Mughal Emperor Akbar's courtesan, but when his son Prince Salim fell in love with her too, Akbar was so enraged that he buried Anarkali alive in a wall located within the bazaar. However, Lahore's supremely romantic and hybrid past constantly rubs against the bathos of financial realities; these are laconically introduced by the US official in the long quotation cited above when he barks, 'And are you on financial aid?'. This is also apparent in Sidhwa's *An American Brat*, in which the young migrant Feroza has all her pride in her education and background in aristocratic Lahore undercut when she tries to enter New York's Kennedy Airport and finds a 'sallow, unsmiling officer' handles her Pakistani passport with contempt, quizzing her on her financial means and the length of time she plans to stay in the USA (Sidhwa 1994, 54).

There are thus barriers to the movement of even the most Mughal-prince-or-princess-like upper-class Lahori, and this suggests the relevance of Michel de Certeau's theorization of 'walking in the city' to an understanding of contemporary Lahore. Writing in 1980, De Certeau lyrically describes the 'ordinary practitioners of the city', who are said to live 'down below', and whose main *raison d'être* is supposed to be *flânerie* or walking. However, interestingly, he begins his account of the ordinary walkers in the city down below from a panoramic vantage point at the top of the World Trade Centre, in a description – which the post-9/11 reader will find chillingly prophetic – of New York as 'a universe that is constantly exploding' (2011, 91) and the World Trade Centre denizen as anticipating 'an Icarian fall' (2011, 92). How can this not resonate with the famous passage in Hamid's *The Reluctant Fundamentalist* in which Changez admits that his first reaction to the twin towers' destruction was to smile, 'caught up', as he was, 'in the *symbolism* of it all, the fact that someone had so visibly brought America to her knees' (2007, 73)?

Once De Certeau descends 'down below' once more, he argues that walking is 'an elementary form of this experience of the city; they are walkers, *Wandersmänner*, whose bodies follow the thicks and thins of an urban "text" they write without being able to read it' (De Certeau [1980] 2011, 93). Yet, Hamid and Sidhwa unsettle these assumptions, showing that walking is not an 'elementary form' in the experience of all cities. In *The Reluctant Fundamentalist*, Hamid writes

> the newer districts of Lahore are poorly suited to the needs of those who must walk. In their spaciousness – with their public parks and wide, tree-lined boulevards – they enforce an ancient hierarchy that comes to us from the countryside: the superiority of the mounted man over the man on foot. But [...] in the [...] congested, maze-like heart of this city – Lahore is more democratically *urban*. Indeed, in these places it is the man with four wheels who is forced to dismount and become part of the city. (Hamid 2007, 33)

Some parts of Lahore are difficult to walk in because they are spread out and lack pavements, while in other places, especially the Walled City areas, the class hierarchy privilege is reversed and it becomes the vehicled person who is at a disadvantage. This is the only instance in Hamid's representations of the divided city where the poor are sometimes privileged over the rich. By contrast to this context-specific privileging, various binaries are set up in his other novels – between the classes who possess air conditioning and their own generators in *Moth Smoke* and those with access to bottled water and those without in *How to Get Filthy Rich in Rising Asia* – which are unvaryingly weighted towards the rich, so the Old City has a levelling effect on class distinctions. De Certeau does mention barriers to movement when he writes of 'interdictions (e.g. [...] a wall that prevents one from going further)' (De Certeau [1980] 2011, 98) – and this becomes much more important in postcolonial cities such as Lahore, with the Wagah border a short car ride away but the partitioned country of India almost impossible to get to for Pakistanis. (It could also be extended to Palestine and the notorious apartheid wall.)

From a gendered perspective, walking in the city is shown to be even more difficult in Sidhwa's *An American Brat*, in which Feroza observes that 'there were so few women, veiled or unveiled, on the streets of Lahore, that even women stared at other women, as she did, as if they were freaks' (Sidhwa 1994, 127). This description of the self-alienation of woman indicates that going outside is a hazardous occupation for her even in one of Pakistan's most sophisticated cities, as she encounters a chasmic gender gap on the streets. In *Cracking India*, Lenny is not only constrained in her walking in the city due to her gender, but also because of her disability. She has suffered polio and is lame, with a fallen arch in one of her feet, and Ayah pushes her in a pram until well past the age for which this is seemly. Once she begins corrective surgery, Lenny worries that her foot will 'emerge [...] immaculate, fault-free', thus forcing her to compete with other children 'for my share of love and other handouts' (1991, 12, 18). In the context of this story concerning Independence, and especially considering that the girl's lameness is arguably an indirect legacy of British rule (1991, 16), it is hard not to read Lenny and her calipers as the infant Indian nation preparing for the difficulties (and rewards) of standing on its own two feet. As Clare Barker writes

> Echoing a problematic conflation of individual and national bodies that was apparent in nationalist discourses in this period, the text becomes a discomfiting oscillation between materialist constructions of disability as a social presence and the deployment of disability as a prosthesis standing in for colonial disablement and mutilated – partitioned – body politic. (2011, 95)

Pakistan as a whole is known to be a hard place for wheelchair users and other disabled people: as well as a lack of ramps and lifts to aid their movement (Farid 2012, n.p.), there is also a widely reported lack of cultural awareness about disability. Further impediments to De Certeau's blithe Western analysis of 'walking in the city' in Lahore include the threat of rape and kidnapping, which becomes a central issue for women during the partition so graphically depicted in *Cracking India*. Moreover, the workers of Heera Mandi are only allowed to move around in their area between 11 pm and 1 am because of draconian and extortive police tactics there.

Conclusion

Perhaps spatial theorists have had a tendency to overlook barriers to walking, particularly when these relate to various forms of oppression in previously colonized countries. Just as there has been a 'spatial turn' in approximately the last three decades of social sciences and humanities research, especially since 9/11 there is increasing interest in analysing the postsecular city (see, for example, Beaumont and Baker 2011; Knott 2010a, 2010b). The idea behind the postsecular turn is to take more account of religion, war and terror's impact on twenty-first-century cities. This is clearly very timely, especially in the light of cities such as Cairo, Benghazi, Damascus, Homs and Hama becoming sites for revolution – to varying degrees religiously inflected – in the Arab Spring of 2011 onwards, so we wait eagerly to see what this new postsecular direction in scholarship will bring to the study of postcolonial cities. In the meantime, it is hoped that this article has shed light on Sidhwa and Hamid's depictions of Heera Mandi's important place within Lahore, itself of inestimable significance to the Punjab and the Pakistani nation.

To conclude, this article has shown that Lahore is a highly multifaceted space, constituted by history, uneven capitalism, rural and urban continuities and discontinuities, and cultural nostalgia. Notwithstanding these noteworthy features, the city is underresearched compared with Indian conurbations (and, to a lesser degree, compared with research into Pakistan's former capital and largest city, Karcachi). As a palimpsest of various accreted histories and the nation's artistic and cultural capital, Lahore is Pakistan's heart (and stomach and spine, to recycle Lieven's metaphor). However, these creative writers from the diaspora construct a complex picture of the city, refuting the binaries that are seductively omnipresent in representations of Lahore. Hamid is keen to dismantle conceptual borders between Lahore and its pastoral hinterland, showing how the city is invading the country in the guise of industrialization, while the country encroaches on the city via the figure of the erstwhile rural denizen seeking a livelihood. Sidhwa adds a gendered dimension to the city in her preoccupation with sex workers in Heera Mandi across almost all of her novels to date. Turning to theory, the article suggested that social science, literary and postcolonial theory provides three broad understandings of space: as a physical reality, a socially constructed entity and a place that is imagined through cognitive mapping and the textualizations of fiction, life writing and non-fiction. Foucault's notion of the heterotopia and de Certeau's walking in the city helps us to see ways in which the city is imagined, but also how its physical manifestations and social manipulations can thwart the imaginer's assumptions and dreams.

Notes

1. However, it should be noted that Hamid returned to live in Lahore in 2009, which may affect the future trajectory of his fiction.
2. The main scholarly monographs on Lahore are Glover (2007) and Suvorova (2012).
3. Both of these incidents, the nuclear race and the Indian parliament attacks, are foregrounded in Hamid's fiction: 2001, 88–92; 2007, 121, 126–127, 143.
4. This term comes from a neglected novel by Markandaya (1982). Heera Mandi is also referred to as a 'Pleasure District' in the subtitle to Louise Brown's book *The Dancing Girls of Lahore* (2006).
5. For further discussion, see Grosz (1990), Butler (1993) and Chiesa (2009).

References

Anjaria, J. S., and C. McFarlane, eds. 2011. *Urban Navigations: Politics, Space and the City in South Asia*. Delhi: Routledge.
Associated Press. 2013. "India, Pakistan Agree: Emotional Google ad a Hit, Strikes a Cultural Chord." *The Hindu*, 15 November. Accessed November 2013. http://www.hindustantimes.com/technology/socialmedia-updates/india-pakistan-agree-emotional-google-ad-a-hit-strikes-a-cultural-chord/article1-1151767.aspx
Bakhtin, M. M. [2004] 1981. *The Dialogic Imagination: Four Essays*, edited by M. Holquist, trans. C. Emerson and M. Holquist, 84–258. Austin: University of Texas Press.
Barker, C. 2011. *Postcolonial Fiction and Disability: Exceptional Children, Metaphor and Materiality*. Basingstoke: Palgrave.
Beaumont, J., and C. Baker, eds. 2011. *Postsecular Cities: Space, Theory and Practice*. London: Continuum.
Brown, L. 2006. *The Dancing Girls of Lahore: Selling Love and Saving Dreams in Pakistan's Pleasure District*. New York: Harper Perennial.
Butler, J. 1993. *Bodies that Matter: On the Discursive Limits of "Sex"*. New York: Routledge.
Chambers, C. 2011. *British Muslim Fictions: Interviews with Contemporary Writers*. Basingstoke: Palgrave.
Chaudhuri, S., ed. 1990. *Calcutta: The Living City: Volume I: The Past*. Delhi: Oxford University Press.
Chaudhuri, S., ed. 1995. *Calcutta: The Living City: Volume II: The Present and Future*. Delhi: Oxford University Press.
Chiesa, L. 2009. "The World of Desire: Lacan between Evolutionary Biology and Psychoanalytic Theory." *Journal of Comparative Literature* 55 (1): 200–225.
Dalrymple, W. 1994. *City of Djinns: A Year in Delhi*. London: Flamingo.
De Certeau, M. [1980] 2011. *The Practice of Everyday Life*, trans. S. Rendell. Berkeley: University of California Press.
Desai, A. 2000. "Passion in Lahore." *New York Review of Books*, 21 December. Accessed November 2013. http://www.nybooks.com/articles/archives/2000/dec/21/passion-in-lahore/
Devi, M. 1995. "Douloti the Bountiful." In *Imaginary Maps: Three Stories*. Translated and edited by intro. G. C. Spivak, 19–94. London: Routledge.
Dutta, K. 2008. *Calcutta: A Cultural and Literary History*. intro A. Desai. Oxford: Signal.
Farid, T. 2012. "Wheelchair Users Deprived of Right to Free Movement." *Daily Times*, 14 January. Accessed April 2014. http://archives.dailytimes.com.pk/lahore/14-Jan-2012/wheelchair-users-deprived-of-right-to-free-movement
Foucault, M. 1980. *Power/Knowledge: Selected Interviews and Other Writings, 1972–1977*. Translated and edited by Colin Gordon, trans. Colin Gordon et al. Hemel Hempstead: Harvester Wheatsheaf.
Foucault, M. 1986. "Of Other Spaces." *Diacritics* 16 (1): 22–27.
Ghosh, A. [1988] 2008. *The Shadow Lines*. Delhi: Penguin.
Glover, W. J. 2007. *Making Lahore Modern: Constructing and Imagining a Colonial City*. Minneapolis: University of Minnesota Press.
Google India. 2013. The Reunion. 15 November. Accessed April 2014. http://www.youtube.com/watch?v=gHGDN9-oFJE
Grosz, E. 1990. *Jacques Lacan: A Feminist Introduction*. London: Routledge.
Gupta, N., S. Mukherjee, and H. Banerjee, eds. 2009. *Calcutta Mosaic: Essays and Interviews on the Minority Communities of Calcutta*. Delhi: Anthem.
Hamid, M. 2000. *Moth Smoke*. London: Granta.
Hamid, M. 2007. *The Reluctant Fundamentalist*. London: Hamish Hamilton.
Hamid, M. 2013. *How to get Filthy Rich in Rising Asia*. London: Hamish Hamilton. Proof copy.

Hansen, T. B. 2001. *Wages of Violence: Naming and Identity in Postcolonial Bombay.* Princeton, NJ: Princeton University Press.
Holston, J., and A. Appadurai. 1999. *Cities and Citizenship.* Durham, NC: Duke University Press.
Hosagrahar, J. 2005. *Indigenous Modernities: Negotiating Architecture, Urbanism, and Colonialism in Delhi.* Abingdon: Routledge.
Jabbar, N. 2011. "Symbology and Subaltern Resistance in Hira Mandi *mohalla*." *Interventions* 13 (1): 95–119.
Jameson, F. 1984. "Postmodernism, or, the Cultural Logic of Late Capitalism." *New Left Review* 146 (July–August): 52–92.
Jameson, F. 1988. "Cognitive Mapping." In *Marxism and the Interpretation of Culture*, edited by C. Nelson and L. Grossberg, 347–357. Basingstoke: Macmillan Education.
Jinnah, M. A. 1994. "An Extract from the Presidential Address of M.A. Jinnah: Lahore, March 1940." In *India's Partition: Process, Strategy and Mobilization*, edited by M. Hasan, 44–58. Delhi: Oxford University Press.
Kaul, H. K., ed. 1997. *Historic Delhi: An Anthology.* Delhi: Oxford University Press.
Knott, K. 2010a. "Religion, Space and Place: The Spatial Turn in Research on Religion." *Religion and Society* 1 (1): 29–43.
Knott, K. 2010b. "Cutting through the Postsecular City: A Spatial Interrogation." In *Exploring the Postsecular: The Religious, the Political and the Urban*, edited by A. L. Molendijk, J. Beaumont, and C. Jedan, 19–38. Leiden: Brill.
Lacan, J. [1981] 1998. *The Four Fundamental Concepts of Psycho-analysis: The Seminar of Jacques Lacan: book xi.* Translated and edited by J-A. Miller, trans. A. Sheridan. New York: Norton.
Lefebvre, H. [1974] 1991. *The Production of Space.* Translated and edited by D. Nicholson-Smith. Oxford: Blackwell.
Le Tournier d'Ison, C. 2012. *Hira Mandi: A Sensitive Portrayal of Life in Lahore's Notorious Centre of Prostitution.* Translated and edited by P. Jhijaria. Delhi: Roli.
Lieven, A. 2011. *Pakistan: A Hard Country.* London: Allen Lane.
Markandaya, K. 1982. *Pleasure City.* London: Chatto & Windus.
Matthews, D. J., C. Shackle, and S. Husain. 2003. *Urdu Literature.* Islamabad: Alhamra.
Mehta, S. 2005. *Maximum City: Bombay Lost and Found.* London: Headline Review.
Pandey, G. 2001. *Remembering Partition: Violence, Nationalism, and History in India.* Cambridge: Cambridge University Press.
Patel, S., and A. Thorner, eds. 1995. *Bombay: Mosaic of Modern Culture.* Bombay: Oxford University Press.
Prakash, G. 2010. *Mumbai Fables: A History of an Enchanted City.* Princeton, NJ: Princeton University Press.
Pratt, M. L. 1992. *Imperial Eyes: Travel Writing and Transculturation.* London: Routledge.
Raju, S., ed. 2011. *Gendered Geographies: Space and Place in South Asia.* Delhi: Oxford University Press.
Rushdie, S. 1988. *The Satanic Verses.* London: Viking.
Saeed, F. 2002. *Taboo!: The Hidden Culture of a Red Light Area.* foreword I. A. Rahman. Karachi: Oxford University Press.
Sidhwa, B. [1980] 1982. *The Crow Eaters.* Glasgow: Fontana/Collins.
Sidhwa, B. 1991. *Cracking India.* Minnesota, MN: Milkweed.
Sidhwa, B. 1994. *An American Brat.* Delhi: Penguin.
Sidhwa, B., ed. 2005. *City of Sin and Splendour: Writings on Lahore.* Delhi: Penguin.
Sidhwa, B. [1983] 2008. *The Pakistani Bride.* Minnesota, MN: Milkweed.
Soja, E. W. 1989. *Postmodern Geographies: The Reassertion of Space in Critical Social Theory.* London: Verso.
Suvorova, A. 2012. *Lahore: Tophophilia of Space and Place.* Karachi: Oxford University Press.
Talbot, I. 1988. *Punjab and the Raj, 1849–1947.* Riverdale, MD: Riverdale Company.
Teverson, A., and S. Upstone, eds. 2011. *Postcolonial Spaces: The Politics of Place in Contemporary Culture.* Basingstoke: Palgrave.
Toor, S. 2011. *The State of Islam: Culture and Cold War Politics in Pakistan.* London: Pluto.
Walder, D. 2011. *Postcolonial Nostalgias: Writing, Representation and Memory.* Abingdon: Routledge.

Culture shock on Southall Broadway: re-thinking 'second-generation' return through 'geographies of Punjabiness'

Kaveri Qureshi

Institute of Social and Cultural Anthropology, Oxford University, Oxford, UK

This paper explores geographies of Punjabiness within Britain in order to engage critically with the recent literature on diasporic return. I begin by drawing attention to the established geographies of Punjabi settlement in Britain, as illustrated by the Thandi coach route maps. This paper considers the significance of these inter-connected hubs of Punjabiness for the multiple identities of the 'second generation'. I examine life history interviews with 'second-generation' Punjabis who grew up in provincial cities and towns off the Thandi route maps – an increasing quantity among Punjabis in Britain. I explore how they construct places like Southall Broadway and Soho Road as Punjabi and go on day trips to these places, as part of their quest for a more authentic identity in the context of their own lives. I show that these places, too, can be crucibles of diasporic nostalgia, exploration of identity and a phenomenological sense of Punjabiness, at times pleasurable and at times unsettling. I suggest that these experiences are akin to diasporic return, speaking to a wider critique about the fetishizing of national borders and the need to decouple diaspora from the idea of originary homelands.

Introduction

Ron Singh, as an 18-year-old college student from Peterborough, had a group of Punjabi friends who he had known since primary school. In their late teens, one of his friends got access to his dad's car, and they decided to leave Peterborough and explore the world outside. It was a classic rite of youthful male exuberance and freedom. And where did they go? Southall Broadway. 'That was such a culture shock, the first time you pull into the street', recalled Ron. 'It's like India, isn't it, especially compared to Peterborough'

This paper takes up the life histories of so-called 'second-generation' British Punjabis, who grew up in provincial cities and new towns across Britain. It looks at what brought them to explore iconic sites of Punjabi settlement like Southall Broadway, what they did in those places, what they made of their experiences and how these trips were significant in their shifting self-identifications. For 'second-generation' British Punjabis growing up in 'White towns', as they call them, going to visit a place like

Southall Broadway seems to offer an experience of 'culture shock' akin to going to the 'ancestral homeland' itself.

'Second generation' is a deeply problematic term that fixes the generations descending from non-White migrants within a racialized 'immigrant imaginary' (Hesse and Sayyid 2006; Kalra 2006). It is a term applied not only to the children but also to the grandchildren of migrants, despite the complexity of tracing generations (for example, the young age at which many Punjabis have come to Britain for family reunification, and the common practice of transnational marriage, which renews a 'first generation' of migrants with every marriage). Given the wide currency of this term among the people with whom I have carried out research, I have retained it in this paper. However, by exploring the multiply placed identities of 'second-generation' British Punjabis I want to pull away from the assumption that Indian Punjab presents an inevitable 'homeland' for people who grow up in the diaspora. This forms part of a wider critique of how 'homeland' functions insidiously as a 'framing device to understand immigration and movement as a cultural prior' (Raj 2003, 166).

In recent years, a literature on 'second-generation' diasporic return has developed. Levitt and Waters's (2003) edited volume establishes 'homeland visits' as an important way for the 'second generation' to renew a sense of attachment to their 'ancestral homeland'. Research with migrant parents has shown how they think about visits 'back home' as a way of actively involving their children in the transnational family (Mason 2004). Similarly, research with 'second generation' has shown how these visits offer a journey of self-discovery and an encounter with their 'roots' (Basu 2004; Coles and Timothy 2004). Visits also offer a phenomenological sense of translocal experience. Migrant parents' longing and fantasies about their 'homeland' are replicated in 'second generation' recollections of visits 'back home' (Wessendorf 2007, 1088), evoking sights, sounds, smells and tastes emanating from accounts tinged with nostalgia (King, Christou, & Teerling 2011, 11), the sensory experience and 'feel' of a place communicating viscerally with memory and identity (Zeitlyn 2013). At the same time, the 'second generation' express a desire for touristic experience 'back home' as well as self-discovery, suffering from boredom in rural areas (McLoughlin and Kalra 1999) – especially young women, who complain about the patriarchal constraints on their mobility and conservatism of their ancestral villages (Bradby 2000) – and experiencing cosmopolitan distance as well as loyalty towards their parents homelands (Bhimji 2008).

However, as Ron tells us, places *within* Britain can also be 'like India'. (Well, "compared to Peterborough"). Instead of the primacy that has been given to movements and relationships across national borders, between places of destination and 'originary homelands', the cultural potency of places like Southall Broadway will require us to map out more complex geographies for diasporic people. The idea of 'translocality' – the connections that are sustained across locales, irrespective of whether they cross national borders – has usefully fractured these bi-focal maps and brought out the plurality of spaces and scales in which migrants and diaspora are emplaced (Brickell and Datta 2011; Datta 2013). In relation to the South Asian diasporas, Kaur and Kalra (1996), inspired by Gilroy's (1993) 'Black Atlantic', propose the term 'Transl-Asia' to decentre the 'originary homelands' and bring out the other 'shifting centres' that come into play as nodes of cultural production. Their model is built on the basis of music produced in Birmingham, and public culture broadcast in Dubai or printed in Toronto. Other authors have dwelled further on the cultural significance of dwelling in or passing through these 'shifting centres'. Sandhya Shukla writes of 'little Indias' like Southall as 'spaces in which, through which, and for which Indianness is being made' (2003, 80). She sees these 'little Indias' as part of a connected map of 'geographies of Indianness' that lead us to re-consider India as an imaginative possibility that exists within and through several nations: 'the directional coordinates become ever less clear ... we can no longer locate the source or the product of Indianness' (Shukla 2003, 16). Similarly, in thinking about the heartlands of South Asian diaspora in Britain, Rajinder Dudrah has drawn attention to the 'spatial "feel"' (2002, 344) that his informants have for 'other centres of South Asian settlement, such as Bradford and Southall, invok[ing] a mental sketch of Britain that illustrates a webbed connection of the British South Asian diaspora up and down the country' (345).

The 'mental sketch of Britain' invoked by the 'second-generation' Punjabis in my research can be illustrated by the Thandi coach route maps.[1] As the name suggests, Thandi coaches is an express coach company established by a Punjabi entrepreneur from Birmingham. Thandi coaches runs daily services between the centres of Punjabi post-migrant populations – Bradford, Wolverhampton, Handsworth, Coventry, Leicester, East Ham, Southall, Ilford, Woolwich and Gravesend – to a primary clientele of married women taking their children to visit their natal families. These are the sites in which Punjabi settlement developed, following chain migration along kinship, marriage and village ties – the latter crossing religious and caste lines. They are *mixed* post-migrant localities. Southall, for example, was a reception town for Welsh and Irish immigrants in the early twentieth century, before attracting Polish, West Indian and South Asian workers after the Second World War. In the 1960s, the dominant stream became Punjabi Sikhs from Jalandhar and Hoshiarpur, before the East African migrations of the early 1970s. Since the 1980s, there have been such growing numbers of Somalis, Black Africans and immigrants from Eastern Europe and the Middle East that many of the Indian Punjabis are moving out, according to Shukla (2003, 123–125). However, the route maps show the *connections between* these sites of widespread Punjabi settlement. In offering passengers the possibility of arriving directly in the Punjabi heartlands, rather than being routed via Victora or Digbeth coach stations, for example, the route maps illustrate the existence of a geography of Punjabi localities in Britain. To emphasize the ethnic particularity I would like to call these 'geographies of Punjabiness' after Shukla, who acknowledges that her term 'geographies of Indianness' submerges regional and religious identities that have their own autonomous diasporas (2003, 18). I invoke the idea of geography not to suggest a fixed physical terrain, but to capture the flow and movement between these 'shifting centres' of settlement, and to convey the embodied, material and affective processes through which places become crucibles for the making of identities (Brickell and Datta 2011; Datta 2013) (Figure 1).

The research participants who feature in this paper should not be identified stably as British Punjabi – a term which, like other ethnic markers, fails to 'fully convey the various and sliding subjectivities that come into play in response to historical, social and political vicissitudes' (Kaur and Kalra 1996, 219). British Punjabi reflects one of multiple possible identity positions that may be assumed, alongside Asian, Indian, Sikh, Bhatra, Jat or Peterborian – 'the question of regional affiliation and the degree of religious and caste consciousness act[ing] as breakable joints' (Kaur and Kalra 1996, 221). Yet, the life histories I explore show how they try to identify something as Punjabi, arching over and above their religious and caste identities. In particular, they idealize particular places as more authentically Punjabi – the 'geographies of Punjabiness' I have laid out above – and make exploratory day trips to them, as part of a

Figure 1. Thandi coaches.

quest for a more authentic identity for themselves, in the context of their own lives (see Marsden (2009), Gill (2012) and Khan (forthcoming) on young men, in different contexts, encountering aspects of identity, ethnic and religious heritage through nostalgic day trips).

The research participants here described the towns and cities in which they grew up as 'White', capturing their experience of minoritization in these places and defying the existence of multicultural enclaves and neighbourhoods within those cities and towns (see Rogaly and Qureshi 2013). Their experiences may be increasingly instructive for the study of Punjabi diasporas in Britain. In the last two decades, flows of internal migration have placed increasing numbers of Punjabi families in sites that are *off* the Thandi route maps. Simpson and Finney (2009) have shown the major pattern for British Indians[2] has been move not to the places of existing concentration, but to new towns, retirement-resort-port areas and mixed urban–rural districts. This reflects, they suggest, the relative prosperity of many Indians compared to other ethnic minority groups, which allows them to move away from inner city areas with greater ease than other minority populations. The context of ethnic concentration that has characterized most research to date – criticized for 'tribalizing' representations of South Asians in Britain (Ahmad 2003, 45) – will increasingly need to be challenged by perspectives from outside the established geographies of settlement.

By looking at the life histories of 'second-generation' British Punjabis who were brought up in provincial cities and towns across Britain, then, and looking at what happened when they encountered the culturally potent 'geographies of Punjabiness' on the Thandi route maps, I suggest that we can usefully re-think the notion of diasporic return. I will develop these ideas through the life histories and embellish on them in the discussion. First, I will provide a brief introduction to the research projects from which the life histories were generated.

Background to the research

This paper draws on two research projects investigating aspects of Indian Punjabi transnationalism, diaspora and translocalism in Britain. The first project, 'Transnet' or 'Transnationalisation, migration and transformation', was funded by the European Commission Seventh Framework Research Programme between 2008 and 2011. It involved research with Punjabi migrants and 'second generation' and sought to explore transnational linkages with Punjab as well as social transformations that have taken place in Britain as a result of long-standing connections with this part of India. I carried out 14 months of ethnographic fieldwork and more than a 100 one-on-one interviews, of which more than 80 were life history interviews with the remainder involving representatives of community and religious organisations. Fifty of the life history interviews were with 'second generation'. The fieldwork was carried out primarily in the West Midlands, East and West London, both heartlands for Indian Punjabis in Britain. In addition, I followed the contacts and interviewed family members and friends in other cities including Gravesend, Bedford, Leicester, Leeds and Bradford. This gave me an immediate 'spatial feel' (Dudrah 2002, 344) for the geographies that I discuss in the paper. I also took photos to convey aspects of those spaces that are hard to explicate in writing, some of which are illustrated here.

The second project, 'Places for all? A multi-media investigation of citizenship, work and belonging in a fast-changing provincial city', was funded by the Arts and Humanities Research Council-led Connected Communities Research Programme between 2011 and 2013 (see www.placesforall.co.uk). It involved research in Peterborough, a small city in the east of England which has a long history of inward migration (both from within the UK and from further afield) due to the pull of its brickworks, engineering and food processing industries. A key interest of the project was the commonality of multiple place attachments for migrants and non-migrants alike (see Rogaly and Qureshi 2013). The project involved residential fieldwork and a core of 76 oral history interviews that Ben Rogaly and I generated with residents in the city. I carried out the majority of the 30 life history interviews with people of South Asian descent, five of which were with Indian Punjabis.

Three life histories

Ron Singh

Ron Singh, born as Rupinder,[3] was born in Peterborough in the late 1960s. His father had come from Punjab to Britain at a very young age, following Partition. Unusually for British Punjabis – except perhaps for Bhatra[4] Sikh families like their own – Ron's father had grown up in a village, rather than a city. He moved from the rural Fens to Peterborough when he was in his late teens. His mother had also come to Britain as a small child and had grown up in the East End of London before moving to Cardiff and then to Bristol. Unlike most of his Asian friends, Ron's parents were themselves brought up in Britain, and they therefore spoke English at home, rather than Punjabi.

Ron remembered the surprise on the face of one of his Asian friends when he once ran into his mother whilst he was out with him in town;

> You wanna hear my mum speak English, it sounds like Julie Andrews [chuckles]. I met one of my friends in town and we were just walking, and my mum came up to us, so my friend said 'Sat sri akaal aunty, kiddan', and that. And my mum said 'I'm very well thank you' [laughter]. And my friend said 'you speak English!' and my mum said 'yes I do!' [chuckles].

Ron spent the early part of his life living in Millfield, the central district of Peterborough that has been a reception area for many generations of new immigrants – a 'contact zone' (Clifford 1997, 17) within a largely White city. Ron remembered Millfield in the 1970s as a happy place where there was so much difference that difference became unremarkable.

> You could walk down the street and first of all you would smell all the different foods that were coming out, you walked past that house there'd be *saag* (greens) just wafting out like that [chuckles]. And then you'd walk past someone else's house and there'd be Polish food and then you'd walk past the Marcus Garvey centre, there'd be Bob Marley playing reggae. And as children all my friends were like Yugoslavian, Chinese, Italian, we all played football together. So we didn't even know there was any difference, and I remember thinking that there was no difference between us at all.

Ron's father and uncle owned the Indian cinema in Peterborough, frequented mainly by the Pakistani immigrants in Millfield. The weekly ritual of going to the gurdwara on Sundays and then going to the cinema was Ron's most regular form of contact with Indianness as he was growing up. He and his siblings could not fully understand the dialogues of those films, with their limited fluency in Hindi and Punjabi.[5] To his mind, this marked them out as not 'proper' Indians. Ron's idea of 'proper' Indians was built up from his observations of family friends and relatives he had seen in other cities; they were not to be found in Peterborough.

> I remember the first time watching *Sholay* with subtitles, thinking you know what, this is a completely different film to the one I watched when I was a kid. Because you just make your own story up, you know who the goody is, you know who the baddy is, and everything is made up in your head. We didn't even know any of the songs. Because we had friends and relatives from other cities, and they were proper Indian, because we weren't really proper Indian, we didn't speak that much Punjabi, we didn't ... we ate Indian food, but they were really hardcore, like no one in their families could speak any English, and they hadn't even heard of Bob Marley, or Elvis.

As a child, Ron never went to India. This was another thing that he felt distinguished his upbringing from that of the friends and relatives elsewhere, those 'proper Indians' who would be going to India for family visits. Ron did, however, have strong memories of going to Bristol in the holidays, to allow his mother to spend some time with her family. Bristol seemed to him a much edgier city than Peterborough. There would be police sirens blaring, fire engines, 'characters' coming into his uncle's shop, his uncle speaking Patois[6] with customers who came in, one of Ron's cousins smoking dope. These were experiences that made him reflect on how provincial Peterborough was. His cousins called him 'bottle breaker' because that was the worst thing he had been reputed to do in his entire life – when they visited Peterborough one year he had broken a bottle, just to give them something to do.[7]

Bristol is just like that, it's really vibrant, it's really chilled and there's always something happening. My cousins would come to Peterborough and they would laugh because they'd say, 'what do you do'? [chuckles] So that's why we were the 'bottle breakers' because there was nothing for them to do here.

Life changed for Ron when he started secondary school and had to cycle out of Millfield and down to Orton Longueville, one of the White 'new towns' in the south of Peterborough that was built in the 1970s to cater to the 'London overspill'. Ron hated secondary school. He and his cousin were the only 'brown' children in the school, in addition to which they had Punjabi names and were wearing *patka*s (topknots). Ron remembered Orton Longueville as the place where he really learnt about racism. When he finished secondary school and went to college, it was therefore a huge relief for him to be reunited with his best friends from junior school in Millfield, a group of them – a Muslim, a Hindu and two Sikhs. One of his friends had access to his dad's car and they went travelling around England, 'just messed around for a year just like ... that's the beauty of being young'. This was their movement of adventure, freedom and fun (see Marsden 2009; Gill 2012; Khan forthcoming). And as I mentioned in the beginning of the paper, the place they chose to go to most of all was Southall. Southall was a place where they found authentic Indianness, 'compared to Peterborough'. They explored the markets, stalls and shops and ate Indian food out at Indian cafés on the Broadway – something you could not do in Peterborough at that time. The look of pleasure that spread over Ron's face as he reminisced about these trips to Southall with his friends spoke volumes (Figure 2).

Figure 2. Moti Mahal on Southall Broadway, West London.

> Just pulled up on Broadway, went for something to eat, because we never ate anything Indian in Peterborough except at home, because there wasn't an Indian restaurant, you couldn't get *gol gappay* (street snacks) or anything in the street. So we'd go to, I think there was a place called Moti Mahal.

It gave Ron a different sense of being Punjabi, a different sense of what it meant to be walking around with brown skin and a turban. In Southall, this was nothing remarkable:

> In Peterborough if you see someone with a turban on you always, *always*, always, have to say hello, 'Sat sri akaal uncle', you'd give them a nod and then they'd give you the nod back, but you acknowledge each other. But now London [chuckles], you never did that. I thought 'these people are really rude, no one's saying hello to me!' [laughter]

His friend the driver was into Southall so much that he ended up moving there – but Ron was more ambivalent. He loved going to Southall too, but preferred the relative calm of Peterborough. The very *feel* of London made him realize how out of place he was there.

> I'm a 'bottle breaker', so just going to London – coming back, you've got black bogies [chuckles] It was just too fast! It was just too fast. You'd come back to Peterborough, it'd be nice.

Balwant Randhawa

Balwant Randhawa was brought up in another 'White town': Reading, a commuter town in Berkshire, about an hour's drive to the West of London. Balwant's father had come to England at the age of eight, to join Balwant's grandfather, who was living in Reading and working as a manual labourer on a farm. Balwant's father had studied in London and then returned to Reading to set up his own business in computer hardware repairs. His mother was born and brought up in Wolverhampton and worked in the civil service. Growing up in a 'White town' in the 1980s, Balwant had few same-age Punjabi friends:

> Reading was primarily – still is – quite a White town. I didn't have any Sikh or Punjabi friends really. I didn't have any growing up, anyway. I guess in a sense I didn't really pick up Punjabi culture until I was older. I really just hung around different sorts of people.

He grew up in the 'contact zone' of Reading: Earley, a neighbourhood just East of the station, not particularly marked by substantial racial or ethnic minorities, but home to the gurdwara and a few Punjabi grocery shops. He described the community in Reading as 'tight': 'even if I might not know a lot of the people, the families will all be aware of each other'. It supported a dappled kind of upbringing in which the Punjabi and Sikh parts of his upbringing seemed to be isolable and separate. They 'didn't do anything cultural' as he was growing up – they would only eat chapati a few times a week, and after Balwant's family moved away from his grandparents' house, they spoke Punjabi so little that he lost the ability to speak it.

> I kind of get a bit uncomfortable around elders who can't speak English, I guess I'm just scared I'll say something wrong so I tend to just sit there being quiet.

IMAGINING PUNJAB, PUNJABI AND PUNJABIAT IN THE TRANSNATIONAL ERA

It was therefore a shock for Balwant when, at the age of 14, they made their one and only family trip to Punjab. Although he enjoyed the trip, it was an experience that made him realize how *un*-Punjabi he was, rather than allowing him to explore his Punjabi identity.

> It was good to see where I came from and where my dad was born and stuff. But I mean, as I was growing up the Punjabi culture wasn't really instilled in me that much so when I went to India I was in a way shocked. I thought this is completely different to what I'm used to, this is not me.

A more formative life experience for Balwant was going back to the West Midlands in the school holidays, to spend time with his mother's family in Wolverhampton. Those summer holidays were focussed on spending time with the family, but he remembered going into town, too, and seeing the big Punjabi presence in the marketplace. He went with his cousins to Sedgely Street gurdwara and was struck by 'just seeing the people there'. Balwant loved Wolverhampton and discovered he had much in common with his cousins with respect to the religion. The town had a flourishing Sikh youth scene with dynamic young preachers who were able to put things 'on the level' in a way that was lacking at his gurdwara in Reading. From Sedgely Street gurdwara, he got involved with a Sikh Camp[8] in the summer holidays. The camp changed his understanding of the religion completely – and made him want to learn more. It was this West Midlands connection, built over many years of summer holidays with his mother's family, that made him want to study in Birmingham:

> I wanted to come to somewhere where there was a decent Sikh community as well, that was one of the major things I looked at. A couple of my aunts live ten minutes from the uni campus in Birmingham so, yeah it kind of helped that I had some family here as well.

Balwant sought out other Indians as soon as he arrived at uni:

> When I actually came to university one of the things – I don't know why I did it, maybe subconsciously or something – but I went to my halls I looked out for Indians basically, I looked out for Asians. Like, I've got quite a mix of friends here, a few of my close friends are White here at university as well, but I've got more Sikh friends like from the Sikh Society and from outside as well.

Although he was staying at a halls of residence on the campus, Balwant said he took himself out of the way to explore the Punjabi parts of Birmingham. He remembered an 'epic night' in which he took a bunch of his friends from uni for a drive along Soho Road:

> I remember just one random night going for a drive just with a couple of friends, just down Soho Road and we'd go to the gurdwara and just have a wander down and see what it was like.

What sort of things struck you about Soho Road?

> Well the first thing you see is the gurdwara, a big, at night just a big blue lit-up building, and then just going down the road and looking at the type of shops there were, the kind of – I guess, even just walking around. It was cool, like, especially compared to what I was used to in Reading.

Down on Soho Road, he and his friends would worship at the Nishkam gurdwara. Then they would wander down and take in the sights and sounds. They would also buy Indian sweets – not because it was a festival or special occasion, but the sight of so many Punjabi shops in such proximity, the sound of *bhangra* music playing from an open car and the hustle and bustle of so many Punjabis would bring out a desire to join in with the action (Figure 3).

He used to go to an Asian night at a club on Broad Street as well and learnt to enjoy the feeling of unrestrained *bhangra* dancing with friends. This too was new to him from Reading:

> Coming from Reading that was really good, cos there's nothing like that in Reading, there's no kind of Punjabi culture there. So going to nights like that was just like – yeah!

Jazz Singh

Jazz Singh was brought up in Basingstoke, a market town in Hampshire that expanded in the 1960s and 1970s to accommodate the 'London overspill'. His mother had migrated to Hounslow as a teenager with her family from Kenya in 1973, and his father had migrated from Punjab in the late 1970s. They had an arranged marriage and moved to Basingstoke in the mid-1980s to take over a post office. Jazz had also grown up without the need to speak much Punjabi, like Ron and Balwant, and lamented his lack of fluency in the language.

Figure 3. Desi Sweet Centre on Soho road, Birmingham.

> I used to speak Punjabi until I was four or five years old, but then a lot of my time was spent with an English childminder and I pretty much forgot most of my Punjabi. Now it's like a fraction of what I knew when I was like, five years old. I can still get by but you know, it's very difficult.

Language skills apart, Jazz felt that his parents had given him a very strong Punjabi Sikh upbringing. He attributed this mainly to his father, who had been politically active in 1970s Punjab and maintained a strong interest in Sikh politics throughout the 1980s. As there was not much going on to that effect in Basingstoke, Jazz's early memories were of being taken across the country to attend gurdwara services and meetings with his father. This had a life-long impact on his political sensibilities. Twenty years on, he still found the symbols, sights and sounds[9] of the gurdwara offered him an uplifting emotional charge.

> *Did you go to temple a lot?*
>
> Oh yeah. Yeah, all over the country when I was a kid, right up til I was six years old. If you go to, I think it's still there, in Southampton, we used to go to Southampton quite a lot and there's a temple there, Nanaksar gurdwara. They actually have Khalistan Zindabad[10] in the main hall. And you know, that was like a radical slogan of Sikh separatism, but there it was, in the main hall.
>
> *Did you enjoy going to those places?*
>
> Yeah, it was awesome. I'm not like a very – my life isn't very strict in terms of my self-discipline and stuff but like, first and foremost I consider myself to be a Sikh. Like nearly all of the music I listen to is Sikh religious music, I've always found it really, you know, it's an integral part of my life.

Growing up in a religious Sikh family in Basingstoke was not easy. He grew up accustomed to being the only Indian in the neighbourhood and the only Indian at school. He described a feeling of 'double consciousness' (Du Bois 2006[1903]), a sense of always looking at himself through the eyes of others, an awareness that his cultural background would be questioned and could not be taken for granted. This was accentuated by wearing a *patka*:

> I had some great times and stuff, but it wasn't easy by any standards. It was quite hard, obviously because I was a brown kid in a very, very, very White area. So it was by no means easy. Also because I have such a strong identity at home, going home in the evening we were a very Punjabi Sikh family – it was like you're literally living two separate lives. And yeah it's quite difficult when you have to then explain why you're different to other people.
>
> *What kind of things would you have to explain?*
>
> Like my hair, firstly. I used to wear a little *patka*, having to explain that, my bracelet, my *kara* (steel bracelet). So yeah that was really the like – probably the biggest part of me has been formed by a very conflictual childhood. I didn't have it as bad as some Asian kids had it, but it certainly wasn't easy.

His difficulties grew when he moved from primary school to secondary school. It was a much larger school, but he was still one of the only racial or ethnic minority students there.

Some of the teachers were good, but it was a very high number of students, about 1500, a very dense school, lots of kids from lots of backgrounds but none of them, to put it really bluntly had ever seen a Paki[11] before. So, it kind of, I found security by hanging out with one of my mates from junior school, his older brother, who was the hardest kid in the school. No one messed with him.

Were you the only South Asian kid in that crowd?

I was probably the only one who was Black or Asian or *anything* in that crowd.

He did not really make very strong friends at secondary school in Basingstoke. The kind of informality that his classfellows enjoyed in friendship, for Jazz, was something he associated with family trips to Hounslow every weekend, undertaken so that his mother could spend time with her family. Jazz's 'buckets of cousins' in Hounslow offered him freedom and fun.[12] Hounslow offered him a chance to explore a different facet of Punjabiness as presented to him via his cousins and their youth culture rather than the adult migrant world of his father and the gurdwara. In his early teens, he started attending a Sikh youth camp at Alice Way gurdwara in Hounslow in the summer holidays. Although he enjoyed the camps, he felt distant from the British Asian youth culture articulated by his friends there and – although he stressed that this reflected his different upbringing, rather than being made to feel like the odd-man-out – it made him realize that he had no understanding of *their* culture (Figure 4).

Did you ever wish that there were Punjabi kids or Sikh kids at school?

No, I just wished people weren't such wankers. That was it really, like, I didn't necessarily identify with the Punjabi kids. I identified with Sikhism, I identified with Punjabi culture, but I didn't identify with a lot of Punjabi kids. At the summer camps, I'd have a wicked time, but I also felt that I'd grown up very differently from them cos they'd grown up in, you know, concentrated areas like Hounslow and Southall, Birmingham. When they got together you could tell that there was this culture that they had, the way that they acted with each other, its informality. When I mixed with them I knew instantly that it was

Figure 4. Alice Way Gurdwara in Hounslow, West London.

something I was part of. I was made to feel a little bit excluded from that. But then that wasn't anything to do with those people, it was just because I had no understanding of their culture. They'd chill with me and I made some great friends, who I see every time I go to Hounslow.

For sixth form, Jazz moved from Basingstoke to a college in Reading, which for him was a significant move as there were more Asian kids in school. He made some Punjabi friends and one of the things he remembered about those friendships was going on trips to Southall.

We used to jump a car with a bunch of mates and go to Southall for an event, like at *Vaisakhi* we'd go for the *nagarkirtan*[13] and then in the evening they'd go out and get mashed! [laughs] In Reading there were more like, Asian areas and you could go to Asian parties in Reading. But Southall, it was more the fact that you're travelling somewhere else, you're going to an area where there's lots of Punjabis, you're seeing a similar culture, but it's different. The times I went with friends it was always quite memorable. In fact, it was a big part of our friendships. It was like going on a holiday abroad with your mates. You're not going abroad but, well, it's almost like you're going abroad.

Jazz was ambivalent about the youth culture he encountered in Hounslow. He was fascinated by it, but at the same time, given the committed upbringing he had been given by his father, he found the youth culture too commercialized and apolitical. He wanted to find something he identified with in it, but it did not provide the right answers for him.

It was a culture shock, especially at first. I always tried to feel a part of it but perhaps because I grew up in such a religious background, in Hounslow it was just basically like British Asian culture, bunch of rude boys, trackies, trainers, listening to drum and bass fusion with *bhangra* and their own street language. But for me the whole Sikh religion and culture is actually heavily entwined with social issues, it comes from a real frustration with the politics of Punjab. So yeah, that melting pot is something to celebrate, but it didn't answer any of the questions that were in my head – the culture, the religious thing I wanted from growing up in a religious Punjabi family, questions about what was there in the world, I had a lot of big questions about the world and about society that I wanted my religion to answer. I looked for that in the British Punjabi youth culture and I didn't find the answers in that either ... You could have a good time but it didn't resonate with what *I* wanted from the culture.

Discussions

These three life histories convey how trips to the heartlands of Punjabi settlement in Britain entered the temporalities of the men's lives in varied ways. All three describe a sense that because of growing up in a 'White town', they somehow were not 'proper' Indians. Perhaps they did not speak much Punjabi, they felt uncomfortable speaking to monolingual Punjabi elders, perhaps they did not eat much Punjabi food, or perhaps they were into Bob Marley rather than *bhangra* music. In the context of their individual lives, they sought a more authentic identity and located that authenticity in an idea of Punjabiness based on observations of family friends and relatives on trips and visits to 'concentrated areas' – to use Jazz's words. Within their idea of Punjabiness, religious and caste differences were unified by culture – language, food, music, including the syncretism of the British Punjabi youth culture. 'Concentrated areas' like Hounslow and Handsworth held a fascination for them. They went out of the way to make trips and visits to these areas and narrated these encounters in accounts laden with enjoyment and nostalgia. These areas offered them a place for them to explore their identities, comparing themselves against the models of Punjabi authenticity they saw before them. The three men took very different meanings from these centres of Punjabiness, sometimes inspired by them, sometimes made to realize their own un-Punjabiness, sometimes disappointed with the hybridized diaspora forms they saw. They experienced a phenomenological sense of Punjabiness – from the sights of shops, stalls purveying street food, the sound of strains of *bhangra* music and so on, to an embodied sense what it feels to be walking around on Southall Broadway with brown skin and a turban. They also fulfil their desire for some kind of touristic experience in these places – consuming services and commodities, snacking on *gol gappay* at an Indian café on Southall Broadway or buying Indian sweets on Soho Road just for the fun of it. Do these centres of Punjabi settlement offer similar journeys of self-discovery as 'homeland visits'? The life histories suggest so. In Jazz's words, 'it's almost like you're going abroad'.

The life histories speak to a wider critique of 'originary homeland' as an inevitable point of return for diasporic people. The notion of diasporic return needs to be expanded so that it is equally capable of dealing with the car-loads of Asian teenagers from small cities and towns who drive to Southall to look at the people, the students who choose Birmingham University so that they can spend three years in a city with a decent Sikh community, and the teenagers who watch their Hounslow counterparts and feel an ambivalent sense of being left out of their mixed-up youth culture. The literature on diasporic return needs concepts to understand the cultural force and energy of places other than the 'originary homeland'. James Clifford advanced a vision of diaspora in which 'decentred, lateral connections are as important as those formed around a teleology of origin/return' (1997, 250). This insight has been extended by concepts such as 'Transl-Asia', which brings out other 'shifting centres' across the spaces of diaspora (Kaur and Kalra 1996), and 'geographies of Indianness' (Shukla 2003), which suggest that India can exist outside its state borders, in these culturally potent ethnic enclaves. Here I have focussed on cultural processes *within Britain*, showing that these 'shifting centres' need not be located across national borders. Within the British Isles, I have discerned 'geographies of Punjabiness' which are idealized as founts of authenticity by 'second generation' in their quest for an authentic identity. It contributes to a growing appreciation of the 'pluri-localities' of diaspora (Brickell and Datta 2011; Datta 2013), and the different embodied, material and affective processes through which people negotiate them in the varied temporalities of their lives.

Acknowledgement

The author is grateful to Ben Rogaly, Filippo Osella and Chand Basi, whose joint work was important to the arguments developed in this paper, as well as to Fatemeh Etemaddar, John Harriss, Niki Khan, Anjali Gera Roy, Ayaz Qureshi and the two anonymous reviewers from *South Asian Diaspora*.

Funding

The research on Punjabi transnationalism was funded by the European Commission Seventh Framework Research Programme under the project 'Transnationalisation, migration and transformation: multi-level analysis of migrant transnationalism'. The research in Peterborough was funded by the Arts and Humanities Research Council, as a part of the Connected Communities

Research Programme, in partnership with the Royal Society and its 'Citizen Power Peterborough' project.

Notes

1. There is now competition among three coach lines offering very similar routes: Thandi coaches, New Bharat coaches and New Punjab coaches. Thandi is the eldest, established in 1985.
2. 'British Indian' is the census category that 'British Punjabis' would use to describe themselves in official statistics. The majority in the 'British Indian' category have Punjabi heritage.
3. Some participants chose for their real-life names to be used in publications extending from the research, whilst others chose a pseudonym, and in other cases, I have given pseudonyms myself.
4. Bhatra is a caste among Sikhs. They are among the earliest Punjabi migrants to Britain, arriving in the early twentieth century to work as pedlars in seaports such as Cardiff and Bristol (Ghuman 1980).
5. Existing sociolinguistic studies of bilingualism among British Punjabis have explored the 'mixed linguistic environments' of British Punjabi socialization and 'imbalanced bilingualism' of the 'second generation' (Romaine 1995; Nesbitt 2000; Martin et al. 2003; Harris 2009). However, all of this research has been carried out in areas of ethnic concentration, raising questions about the extent to which linguistic proficiency might be affected by the ethnic density of the wider communities in which children grow up.
6. 'Patois' describes the language forms of West Indian-origin diaspora in Britain.
7. See Corrigan (1979) on young men smashing milk bottles on the pavements of Sunderland in the 1970s.
8. See Singh (2011) for a history of the Sikh camps that had developed in Britain by the early 2000s.
9. See Jacobsen (2012) on the integral role of devotional music in Sikh experience and identity.
10. Long live 'Khalistan', the separatist state fought for by Sikh ethno-nationalists in the 1970s–1990s.
11. 'Paki' is the epithet used most widely in racist name-calling against South Asians in Britain.
12. See Baumann (1995) on the 'cousin-brother' category as a means to transgression among youth in Southall.
13. 'Vaisakhi' is a spring festival celebrated across North India, with particular resonance for Sikhs, as it commemorates the birth of the Khalsa in 1699. Vaisakhi is celebrated by the practice of 'nagarkirtan', which is a congregational procession, bearing the Guru Granth Sahib, conducted amid devotional music.

References

Ahmad, F. 2003. "'Still in Progress?': Methodological Dilemmas, Tensions and Contradictions in Theorizing South Asian Muslim Women." In *South Asian Women in the Diaspora*, edited by N. Puwar and P. Ranghuram, 43–65. Oxford: Berg.

Basu, P. 2004. *Highland Homecomings: Genealogy and Heritage-Tourism in the Scottish Diaspora*. London: Routledge.

Baumann, G. 1995. "Managing a Polyethnic Milieu: Kinship and Interaction in a London Suburb." *Journal of the Royal Anthropological Institute* 1 (Dec): 725–741.

Bhimji, F. 2008. "Cosmopolitan Belonging and Diaspora: Second-Generation British Muslim Women Travelling to South Asia." *Citizenship Studies* 12 (4): 413–427.

Bradby, H. 2000. "Locality, Loyalty and Identity: Experiences of Travel and Marriage among Young Punjabi Women in Glasgow." In *Tourism and Sex: Culture, Commerce and Coercion*, edited by S. Clift and S. Carter, 236–249. London: Cassells.

Brickell, K., and A. Datta, eds. 2011. *Translocal Geographies: Spaces, Places, Connections*. Aldershot: Ashgate.

Clifford, J. 1997. *Routes: Travel and Translation in the Late Twentieth Century*. Cambridge, MA: Harvard University Press.

Coles, T., and D. Timothy. 2004. *Tourism, Diasporas and Space*. London: Routledge.

Corrigan, P. 1979. "Doing Nothing." In *Resistance through Rituals: Youth Sub-Cultures in Post-War Britain*, edited by S. Hall and T. Jefferson, 103–105. London: Routledge Kegan and Paul.

Datta, A. 2013. "Diaspora and Transnationalism in Urban Studies." In *A Companion to Diaspora and Transnationalism*, edited by A. Quayson and G. Daswani, 88–105. Oxford: Blackwell.

Du Bois, W. E. B. 2006[1903]. *The Souls of Black Folk*. Pennsylvania: Pennsylvania State University.

Dudrah, R. 2002. "Birmingham (UK): 'Constructing City Spaces through Black Popular Cultures and the Black Public Sphere.'" *City* 6 (3): 335–350.

Ghuman, P. A. S. 1980. "Bhatra Sikhs in Cardiff: Family and Kinship Organisation." *New Community* 8 (3): 308–316.

Gill, H. S. 2012. *Becoming Men in a Modern City: Masculinity, Migration and Globalization in North India*. Washington, DC: American University.

Gilroy, P. 1993. *The Black Atlantic: Modernity and Double Consciousness*. London: Verso.

Harris, R. 2009. *New Ethnicities and Language Use*. London: Routledge.

Hesse, B., and S. Sayyid. 2006. "Narrating the Postcolonial Political and the Immigrant Imaginary." In *A Postcolonial People: South Asians in Britain*, edited by N. Ali, V. S. Kalra and S. Sayyid, 13–31. London: Hurst.

Jacobsen, K. 2012. "Tuning Identity in European 'Houses of the Guru': The Importance of Gurdwaras and *Kirtan* among Sikhs in Europe." In *Sikhs across Borders: Transnational Practices of European Sikhs*, edited by K. Myrvold and K. Jacobsen, 105–118. London: Bloomsbury.

Kalra, V. S. 2006. "Ethnography as Politics: A Critical Review of British Studies of Racialized Minorities." *Ethnic and Racial Studies* 29 (3): 452–470.

Kaur, R. and V. Kalra. 1996. "New Paths for South Asian Identity and Musical Creativity." In *Dis-Orienting Rythyms: The Politics of the New Asian Dance Music*, edited by S. Sharma, J. Hutnyk and A. Sharma, 217–231. London: Zed Books.

Khan, N. forthcoming. "The Taste of Freedom: Commensality, Liminality and Return Amongst Afghan Transnational Migrants in the UK and Pakistan." *Journal of the Royal Anthropological Institute*.

King, R., Christou, A., & Teerling, J. 2011. "We Took a Bath with the Chickens': Memories of Childhood Visits to the Homeland by Second-Generation Greek and Greek-Cypriot 'Returnees'." *Global Networks* 11 (1): 1–23.

Levitt, P., and M. Waters, eds. 2003. *The Changing Face of Home: The Transnational Lives of the Second Generation*. New York: Russell Sage.

Marsden, M. 2009. "A Tour Not So Grand: Mobile Muslims in Northern Pakistan." *Journal of the Royal Anthropological Institute* 14 (Supplement s1): S57–S75.

Martin, D., R. Krishnamurthy, M. Bhardwaj, and R. Charles. 2003. "Language Change in Young Panjabi/English Children: Implications for Bilingual Language Assessment." *Child Language Teaching and Therapy* 19 (3): 245–265.

Mason, J. 2004. "Managing Kinship over Long Distances: The Significance of 'the Visit'." *Social Policy and Society* 3 (4): 421–429.

McLoughlin, S., and V. S. Kalra. 1999. "Wish You Were(N't) Here: Discrepant Representations of Mirpur in Narratives of Migration, Diaspora and Tourism." In *Travel-Worlds: Journeys in Contemporary Cultural Politics*, edited by J. Hutnyk and R. Kaur, 120–136. London: Zed Books.

Nesbitt, E. 2000. *The Religious Lives of Sikh Children: A Coventry Based Study.* Leeds: Monograph Series, Community Religions Project.

Raj, D. S. 2003. *Where Are You From? Middle-Class Migrants in the Modern World.* Berkeley: University of California Press.

Rogaly, B., and K. Qureshi. 2013. "Diversity, Urban Space and the Right to the Provincial City." *Identities: Global Studies in Culture and Power* 20 (4): 423–37.

Romaine, S. 1995. *Bilingualism.* Oxford: Blackwell.

Shukla, S. 2003. *India Abroad: Diasporic Cultures and Postwar America and England.* Princeton: Princeton University Press.

Simpson, L., and N. Finney. 2009. "Spatial Patterns of Internal Migration: Evidence for Ethnic Groups in Britain." *Population, Space and Place* 15 (1): 37–56.

Singh, J. 2011. "Sikh-Ing Beliefs: British Sikh Camps in the UK." In *Sikhs in Europe: Migration, Identities and Representations*, edited by K. Jacobsen and K. Myrvold, 253–278. Aldershot: Ashgate.

Wessendorf, S. 2007. "'Roots Migrants': Transnationalism and 'Return' among Second-Generation Italians in Switzerland." *Journal of Ethnic and Migration Studies* 33 (7): 1083–1102.

Zeitlyn, B. 2013. "Making Sense of the Smell of Bangladesh." *Childhood.* doi:10.1177/0907568213488965.

Punjabiyat and the music of Nusrat Fateh Ali Khan

Virinder S. Kalra

Department of Sociology, University of Manchester, Manchester, UK

Undoubtedly, one of the most popular singers of South Asia, Nusrat Fateh Ali Khan, individually, and as part of his Qawaali party has been neglected in the academic literature. Rectifying that situation, this article locates his biography and music in the context of another under-theorised area of scholarly work, that of *Punjabiyat*. In exploring Nusrat's biography, the connections between a non-essential notion of *Punjabiyat* and musical performativity are illustrated and examined. The various forces that operate to sustain musical and cultural continuity are presented in an oscillation between the normatively demarcated zones of East Punjab, West Punjab and the Punjabi diaspora.

Par par aalam faazal hoya
Kadee apne aap nu parheya nay
Ja ja warda Mandir maseeti
Kadee apne aap wich warrya nay
Ehvain roz Shaitaan naal larda
Kadee nafs apnay naal larrya nay

Reading the texts you became a scholar
You never managed to read your self
Rushing into the Mandir and Mosque
You never entered your own heart
Fighting with the devil pointlessly
You never challenged your own ego.[1]

(Attributed to Bulleh Shah as rendered by Nusrat Fateh Ali Khan and Party 'Ni Mai Jaan Jogi de naal,' 'I am going with the Jogi')[2]

Since Nusrat Fateh Ali Khan's (NFAK's) untimely death in 1997, his reputation and popularity does not seem to have waned. Indeed, whilst many members of the original Qawaali party also passed on, his nephew, Rahat Fateh Ali Khan continues to sing the families repertoire to critical acclaim. In Pakistan and North India, almost all Qawaali groups sing at least one 'Nusrat number' when performing live and many have re-recorded various parts of the NFAK repetoire. Nusrat's style has been imitated with artists such as Hans Raj Hans (formerly a folk singer) taking up the mantle of a commercially successful, 'Sufi Music' (Manuel 2008). In Britain, the musical impact of NFAK continues to be felt. In 2013, the *BBC* aired a two-part radio documentary titled 'Guru of peace' documenting the singers life and featuring perspectives from a range of artists discussing Nusrat's influence on their own work.[3] Indeed, from the evidence of Youtube views and record sales,[4] NFAK still maintains a strong presence in the world music scene and amongst South Asian diasporic artists. The range and depth of the eulogies in the BBC radio documentary bear further testimony to the legacy. Despite this prominence, his life and musical contribution have been relatively neglected in musicological studies of Qawwali and in general cultural studies accounts relating to South Asian culture. Though by no means a comprehensive redress to this situation, the intention here is to present NFAK's family and musical biography to explore two aspects of a varied and complex career. First, the role that he played in reflecting a common Indo-Pak cultural terrain, most prominently, perhaps, in his work in Bollywood – singing on film tracks – but more intensely in the Punjab. It is this latter cultural work that is, I will argue, most usefully conceptualised in terms of the notion of *Punjabiyat* and perhaps most potently performed in the Qawwali, *Ni mai jana jogi de naal*, attributed to Bulleh Shah and one of the tracks on Nusrat's first studio recordings.[5] The second issue of concern is the way in which this notion of musical *Punjabiyat*, as represented by NFAK, is one (perhaps the only) key way in which the Punjabi diaspora is able to frame itself outside of dominant fractures of religion, caste and nation.[6] Indeed, writing the Punjabi diaspora requires a double undoing of the national narrative, implicit when diaspora is evoked but more prominent when the group in question is itself split across two nation-states (Kalra, Ibad, and Purewal). These two issues by no means exhaust the rich source of musicological and cultural insight that NFAK provides, rather they are indicative and hopefully generative of further analysis.[7]

Studies of the Punjabi diaspora as a specific entity are few and far between, rather the existing literature is dominated by a methodological hierarchy that prioritises the nation-state as the basic unit of analysis disaggregating to religious groups (Wimmer and Glick Schiller 2002). Thus, numerous volumes cover topics such as the Indian diaspora or Sikhs in Britain or South Asian Muslims all of which contain elements of what might putatively be called a Punjabi diaspora.[8] Depending on starting point, East or West Punjab (India or Pakistan), the other is left out of the analysis and to compensate, for this absence, greater attention is made to other aspects of identity such as religion. Though there are certainly clear arenas such as that of marriage or piety in which a singular focus on caste or religion would make entire sense, sites of Punjabi commonality based on language and culture are neglected.[9] Perhaps, the trajectories of the nation-states of India and Pakistan are sufficiently divergent to make the case that difference not commonality is the better way of viewing Punjabis settled in diasporic settings. This would perhaps be to overly privilege the impact of the postcolonial states on intellectual debate, rather the institutional contexts in which diaspora and immigration are studied are closely related to and derive from a historical perspective on Punjab which focuses on discrete religious groups and communities. In a strident critique of the state of academic scholarship on Punjab in Indian Universities, Surinder Singh and Ishwar Gaur describe it as 'Sikh-centric'.[10] The result of which is a ' ... dispensation [that] refuses to conceive Punjab as a region which experienced a specific socio-cultural evolution. It views the eighteenth century as a Sikh–Muslim (religious) conflict' (Singh and Gaur 2009, 33). They go on to examine the development of the history syllabus and conclude that a student of medieval Punjab would have little to no knowledge of the role of Sufis in the making of the social and cultural orders. In parallel, the role of non-Muslims is either ignored or viewed negatively in history books in

Pakistan.[11] In summary, where the Punjab is most studied as an entity, it is almost entirely through a lens which focuses on the role of Sikhs. Thus, embracing the logic of colonial conflation of religion with language and culture (Mandair 2009). The formula being, Urdu:Muslim:Pakistan, Hindi:Hindu:India and Punjabi:Sikh:?. The question mark being subsequently filled by the call for Khalistan. It is this logic that betrays itself in much of the literature on the South Asian diaspora which attempts some focus on Punjabis. Boundaries and borders are as much maintained by scholarship as they are disrupted. There are Sikh studies Chairs in Universities in America, Iqbal Fellows at the University of Cambridge and Oxford and a plethora of departments devoted to the study of Islam. Yet there is no single department or research centre which attempts to consider Punjab in its totality. The parochial nature of academic institutions in East Punjab, with portentous names such as Punjabi University only belies there deep embodiment within Sikh hegemony, at the local state level.[12]

A significant attempt at moving beyond this colonial conflation of language and religion erected is offered in the edited collection by Malhotra and Mir (2012). Utilising the idea of cultural history as a way of (re)connecting the disparate national/religious boundaries that keep apart potential commonalities, the editorial introduction to the book *Punjab Reconsidered* foregrounds the shifting and multiple terrain that encompasses a useful conceptualisation of *Punjabiyat*. For Malhotra and Mir, this is a: 'loosely defined term often used to describe a sentiment of belonging or attachment to Punjab and/or the foundations of shared, cross-religious, cross-caste, cross-class culture' (2012, xv). It is the latter definition that is of most interest in the present context and rather than viewing *Punjabiyat* as a classification it is, like the term diaspora, used here as a critical tool with which to interrogate claims to exclusivity and bounded identities. It is at the level of creative expression that this reading of *Punjabiyat* is most visible and it is therefore no coincidence that it is those chapters in the book *Punjab Reconsidered* that focus on culture, where boundaries begin to overlap and merge and the conceptualisation of *Punjabiyat* as a critical tool emerges. It is in the sphere of culture that the contribution of NFAK, as part of his Qawaali party and in his individual musical contribution, can be most usefully located. Ostensibly connected to the tradition of Qawaali that is associated with the shrine of Nizamuddin Auliya in New Delhi, NFAK's popularity with an international audience only served to enhance his placement within a particular rendering of *Punjabiyat*. Rather than abandon his roots as he emerged as a 'World music' and Bollywood star, he sought to embellish and enhance them via a routing in his families musical tradition. This diasporic Punjabi imaginary emerges from the traumas of partition as well as the attempt at healing that rupture through musical continuity. In that sense, it is not migration to the West that instantiates a diasporic consciousness and sensibility in NFAK, but a recognition that his musical tradition is open to a certain kind of translation that is already tested by the India/Pakistan border and which would subsequently appeal to a Punjabi diasporic audience. In that sense, NFAK transcends any narrow notion of *Punjabiyat*, as his music always appealed to a wide(r) audience. These issues are explored via a biography of Nusrat drawn from popular texts and a series of interviews he gave to various television channels in the 1980s and 1990s. These vignettes serve as markers from which an exploration of the concept of *Punjabiyat* in relation to music is undertaken.

Partitions of music
Hailing from a small village, Basti Sheikh, now part of Jalandhar city, NFAKs' family were already well known as reputable Qawaals in pre-partition Punjab. Whilst they

were not affiliated musically with one shrine, their family Pir's *dargah* was Tala Sharif, near Dasua, Hoshiarpur and the family belonged to the Sabri-Chisti order. Like many other Qawwal groups, they made their living primarily from performing on Thursday evening's at shrines; at the annual Urs/mela celebrating the death anniversary of the Pir; and at private functions. It was the changing political environment in Punjab, from the late 1930s onwards, that had the main impact on Fateh and Mubarek's, Nusrat's father and elder uncle, respectively, musical practices. In the turbulent political climate, the brothers became involved in the development of *Iqbaliat*, which were songs inspired by Allama Iqbal's poetry, and created to support the political campaigning of the Muslim League (Qureshi 1992/1993; Baud 1996). Indeed, one of the stories about the pre-partition family relates to how Hindus were desperate for the brothers to stop singing their propaganda for Pakistan as their musical talent was harnessing so much support for the Muslim League (Baud 2008). In the same period, Bombay Qawaals were, in contrast, increasingly singing heterodox and Indian-centred Sufi texts, in support of the Indian National Congress (Qureshi 1992/1993).[13] Like so many other of the Punjabi Qawaal groups, during partition, the family moved from Jalandhar to Lyallpur (Faislabad) and re-established themselves in the new nation. In keeping with their dual engagements, they lived near the shrine of Lasoori Shah, in the central city of Lyallpur, and this is where NFAK first performed. At the same time and perhaps due to their affiliation with the Muslim league, the brothers Mubarak and Fateh Ali were able to gain lucrative employment as Radio Pakistan grade A musicians. Despite this engagement with the world of radio and studios, they did not undertake any commercial recording and never produced a studio tape.[14] This should not indicate a static response to the music or changing times, as the development of *Iqbaliat* Qawaali demonstrates. Indeed, their migration from Jalandhar into postcolonial Lyallpur and the need for a national music for Pakistan led to them develop the Qawaali genre for specific types of state sponsored public performance (Rubi 1992).

Dominant accounts of Qawaali locate it either within the broader Islamic-Sufi musical world, stretching from Syria through to Indonesia (Frembgen 2008) or in the long historical line of a 700-year-old tradition based at Nizamuddin's shrine in Delhi (Qureshi 1995). The scholarly neglect of Punjabi Qawaali in this context may be due to the process, pithily described by Jacoviello: 'the original spiritual genre underwent both a process of desecration in Punjab and a process of profanation on its way to the West. "Desecration" means the progressive loss of sacred value' (2011, 325). Contemporary accounts, keen to locate Qawaali within the format of 'tolerant' Islam are unable to undertake the jarring journey to Punjab, where the boundaries between folk and religious music, in their blurring imply a 'desecration'. In the final shift to the diaspora, the genre loses all connection to (religious) origins and is rendered into a commercial, commodity. This critique of Nusrat's music was made perhaps most poignantly by Lahore-based film-maker, Farjad Nabi, in the documentary: 'Nusrat has left the building ... but when'.[15] Yet these readings of NFAK are deeply entrenched in a narrative of authenticity that any, even superficial, understanding of the context of Qawaali and in particular NFAK's role within the genre would find difficult to sustain (Kalra 2014). The issue of 'authentic' Qawaali form has provided ample opportunity for confusion. For example, in pioneering research, Sakata (1994) analyses the performances of over 20 concerts that NFAK's group gave in a variety of Pakistani and diasporic contexts.[16] The conundrum for the music professor simply being the extent to which Qawaali can be seen as a spiritual music, even though what might convey this religious element is not clear from contexts of performance or the often ambiguous lyrical content. In breaking down sites of performance into either sacred and secular, Sakata (1994) concludes that it is not clear from the context which behaviour might match the distinction established by Qureshi (1986) between religious and commercial Qawaali.[17] Rather, Sakata (1994) argues, Nusrat's performance in the sacred setting of the *Urs* of Data Sahib in Lahore is more demotic and carnivelesque than at the secular state sponsored Lok Virsa Institute in Islamabad. It is the audience that determines the mood in both cases. Indeed, the most sober and attentive audience was that at Washington University, where the concert audience was the most mixed in terms of religion, ethnicity and gender. In a sense, the Western context provides the most religious context (where sobriety is defined as religious) and the Lahori the most demotic. In an in-depth interview,[18] with the Lok Virsa Institute in 1989, Nusrat himself presents the *music* as the main appeal to non-South Asian audiences, which is logical given that they would not understand the texts and that it is the emotions present in the music which are the attraction *and* the message.[19] It is this approach to the music which provides the consistency across the various contexts in which he performs, rather than any identification of sacred and secular. It is this difficulty of classification, perhaps, which may also account for NFAK's absence in accounts of Sufi music or in historiographies of Qawwali.

Nusrat reflects on his own music outside of static definitions and binaries, for example, making a much softer and fluid distinction between the religious and secular stating that there are 'soulful' and 'romantic' moods which are reflected in the performance.[20] Even the international stature that NFAK rose to is related by him back to the world of popular spirituality in the Punjab, rather than to any long tradition. As he states: 'Whatever I am, is due to the grace and faith of these elders (*buzorgoan*), I am nothing of myself, it is all their doing. Following in their footsteps is my duty' (NFAK in Baud 2008, 25).[21] It is 'elders', in the specific sense of Nusrat's father and uncle, who also provide the other site for Nusrat's legitimacy in the world of Qawwali. Many Qawwals in contemporary Punjab trace a musical lineage that stretches back four to five generations, but of more contemporary significance attempt to establish a connection with NFAK's family.[22] Locating NFAK in the context of Faislabad, West Punjab and Pakistan might lead to a framing that evokes partition, Islamic ideology and anti-Indian nationalism. Considering NFAK's considerable musical output an indication of some of these strands can certainly be found.[23] However, it is also clear from the circulation of his music in North India and from the videos of his concerts performing in the UK that his appeal transcended the confines of religion and nation. In particular, when performing Punjabi tracks, he certainly appealed to and arguably enabled the evocation of *Punjabiyat*. It is the affective role that NFAK's music played which enables a critical assertion of *Punjabiyat*, a role that is exemplified by Singh and Gaur in their volume on Sufism: 'Essays in the present volume constitute a "transgressive" text in the sense that they transcend the conventional boundaries and communitarian standards of writing the history of Punjab' (2009, 35). Nusrat's music is able, in the absence of cross-border transnational, political or social movements and institutions, to slip through the gaps of border control initially via cassette copying and now via digital technologies.[24] In her insightful book, *Bhangra Moves*, Roy makes a similar argument: 'In the process of engaging with the variety of subject positions it unfolded, Punjabiyat is transformed. The Panjabi identity constructed in relation to Bhangra disengages ethnicity from nation and religion and returns it to language, region, culture and the body. Unlike Sikh nationalism, which

South Asian Diaspora mobilised religion and language to appropriate Punjabiyat for sikhi, Bhangra Nation manipulates primordial ties attached to the bioregion, biology and everyday conduct and rituals in reaffirming an inclusive Punjabiyat' (2010, 222). In the broader cultural domain, *Punjabiyat* is (ab)used in different ways, for example, in the bedazzling, commoditised world of Bollywood movies, Punjabis are sometimes represented through the valorisation of upper caste/class Khatri business families, marginalising Sikhs and dalits and sometimes through the figure of the male, turbaned, bearded Jat Sikh. This latter hypermasculine figure comes in the form of the bhangra dancer, the warrior and ultimately the Indian soldier. A similar bifurcation between neglect and caricature is also present in Pakistan where the 'true' Punjabi is considered to be the Jat male with accompanying values of loyalty, erratic but passionate emotions and unbridled masculinity.[25] Conversely, the disregarding of Punjabi can be seen in the presentation of Qawwali on Pakistan (public and private) television channels where only Urdu and Farsi texts are broadcast.[26] It is therefore a specific framing of Bhangra that offers a space for *Punjabiyat* to do the work of subverting national boundaries and unifying sectarian divides.[27] This critical use of the concept does not belie its lived sense as Malhotra and Mir succinctly state:

> We have not only empahasised the amorphous ad shadowy nature of our nodal idea of Punjabiyat, but also underlined that for all its ambiguity, the notion is real in so far as it exercises people's imaginations, emotions, experiences and sense of self. (2012, Ii)

But it is necessary to be careful when considering this 'real' aspect of Punjabi identity as it is equally able to be utilised for narrow, sectarian politics as for cosmopolitan border crossings. *Punjabiyat*, as a critical tool specifically refers to the oscillation between that which is rooted in tradition and routed through creative engagement. This conceptualisation is usefully evoked in the way in which Nusrat placed his own music in relation to its past.

In a series of interviews given from 1989 to 1999, Nusrat develops a musical lineage which brings together the two great strands of music related to Moghul patronage in the sub-continent: Dhrupad and Qawwali. In one of his first extensive interviews with the Lok Virsa Institute, in Islamabad, he talks about his *gharana* tracking a lineage to Behram Khan and to the *Dagar Bani* of Dhrupad.[28] This relationship to tradition is not static as it is clear that NFAK's father and uncle were successful precisely because they were able to respond to the changing climate in British India. In that sense, Nusrat's forays into the world of commercial recording and ultimately into the world of film (Hollywood and Bollywood) is continuous with practices of innovation. Nusrat maintains that the tradition of Qawaali retains an ideal place, which given the stature of Mubarak and Fateh Ali, for him could not be matched. The changes that NFAK's group bought about were therefore different to the inherited tradition but nonetheless maintained integrity.[29] NFAK's initial innovations in Pakistan were to introduce folk notation and to change the ways in which notes were expressed, often resulting in faster beats and punchier melodic lines. These musical changes followed from shifts in instrumentation in North Indian music as a whole from the use of *Sarangi* and *Shenai* at the beginning of the twentieth century to violin and clarinet by the middle and then to the hegemony of the harmonium. Thus, introducing other western instruments and studio sampled sounds were not outside of the continuous processes of change which were part of Nusrat's musical upbringing. This change is not expressed in terms of decay or decline by Nusrat but rather as central to three socio-musical projects.

First, in the Pakistani context, the desire to attract a wider audience to Qawaali, which he perceived was lacking due to the overtly classical nature of the musical offerings. Second, in the South Asian diaspora to enable a connection, for Punjabis in particular to the stories of *Heer Ranjha* and other epic love poems. Finally, to make his music appealing to an international musical public, he sang in many different genres, such as world music and bollywood.[30] These reflections on musical practice were fundamentally informed by Nusrat's success in Europe and North America.

Coming to London

If partition of British India instigated a division of people that fragmented and fissured a common sense of *Punjabiyat*, then ironically migration to the imperial homeland recreated that lost social space. In the factories, mills and foundries of 1960s urban Britain, male workers from India and Pakistan found commonality in the songs of Hindi film and the folk tunes of Punjab. As part of the development of urban diasporic spaces, shops selling music became a feature of inner-city high streets throughout the UK (Dudrah 2010). Ayub Khan, owner of Oriental Star Agencies, one of the first retail outlets for South Asian music in Britain, relates his first encounter with NFAK:

> In 1978, a friend of mine from London, Haji Rayatullah, who used to bring music for me from Pakistan ... bought a recording for me (on big reel to reel spools) and said you must listen to this. When I heard it, I felt like the voice of the soul has come into my heart. I felt like I was listening to a voice that would one day become famous throughout the world. From that day, I wanted to bring this voice, that of Nusrat Fateh Ali Khan to the world.[31]

In 1979, NFAK came to Birmingham for the first in a series of concerts, which took place in various halls and sometimes Public houses (very appropriate *mehkhanas*).[32] The group's first, video recorded, concert took place in the Luxor Cinema in Birmingham and subsequently NFAK performed regularly in the UK at public and private functions. In these early concerts, NFAK was deeply integrated into the local domains in which the lines between the cultural and the political, the social and the economic were fuzzy. For example, a musical performance, a public meeting or a religious event were not so spatially segregated in this time. In 1985, NFAK performed at the Farcroft Public House in Handsworth in Birmingham. This was the same year that public disturbances, of migrant youth against the police, raged through the area (Cottle 1994). The Farcroft itself was the venue where the Indian Workers Association, a long-standing institution fighting for social justice as well as communal harmony, held public meetings (Gill 2013). It is not surprising that in these spaces, Nusrat's repertoire would extend beyond the Qawaali genre to engage with other spiritual music texts, such as devotion to *Mata devi* or in praise of Kabir.[33] The interaction across religious boundaries was enabled by the diasporic context (unlike postcolonial Punjab) and thus in 1989, NFAK performed at Slough Gurdwara, near London, singing texts from the Sikh tradition.[34] The space of diaspora created the conditions to re-imagine a nineteenth-century Punjab in which the role of musicians was not delimited by their religious identity, rather they were the main purveyors of what Mir (2010) has termed a parallel piety, but I would label *Punjabiyat*. In 1980s Britain, NFAK was clearly capable, despite being born in post-partition Lyallpur of engaging in a range of genres encompassing Sikh, Hindu and Muslim musical traditions. This inter-religious diasporic music space also emerges in another version of Ayub Khan's first encounter with NFAK that he related in another interview:

> I remember we were three people in that room. Me, my brother and Sam Sagoo ... and we put this reel on and all of a sudden everyone was mesmerised when we heard that first take, 'Haq Ali Ali'. That was Nusrat's first introduction to us and I thought this is a wonderful energy and voice, which we must introduce to the world. The world should benefit from this great singer.[35]

The purpose of repeating another version of this story is to note the presence of Sam Sagoo in this physical musical entry of NFAK into 1970s Birmingham. Oriental Star Agencies offices provide us with another imaginary: the studios of All India Radio in Jalandhar in the 1930s, where Punjabi musicians, regardless of religious background interacted in the creation of new musical forms, in response to the new technologies of recording and transmission. Sam Sagoo is the father of Bally Sagoo, one of the leading early producers of a distinctive British Bhangra sound, who would go onto record Nusrat in the 1991 album *Magic Touch*. Sam Sagoo still DJs on a radio station and at one point owned an Indian music shop, but it is Bally Sagoo's relationship that exemplifies the way in which NFAK crossed generations in terms of his appeal. In an interview after NFAK's death, Bally Sagoo tells:

> I knew about Nusrat, but had not heard his music or knew much about it. [By this time, Bally Sagoo had recorded some best selling bhangra remix albums]. When he came to the studio, he just sat down and in two hours recorded vocals for six tracks. No arrangement or anything ... .After the album was complete I became a big fan and so did lots of other kids who heard it for the first time ... Everywhere you went young people were playing Magic Touch, in cars, in colleges, clubs ... [36]

The diasporic story about the importance of the musical culture that developed in the UK in the 1980s has been well examined (Sharma, Hutnyk, and Sharma 1996; Dudrah 2007; Roy 2010). This has mostly been a sociological story couched in the language of youth subculture and identity but not as much attention has been paid to the musical cross-fertilisation that the diasporic context enabled. Bally Sagoo, Malkit Singh and a range of artists from East Punjab, East Africa and West Punjab were given the opportunity to interact with Nusrat through the auspices of Oriental Star Agencies. This led to a number of remixes of NFAK's music, primarily with dance music but it also provided a space for East and West Punjab to meet and for Sufi, Bhakti and Gurbani textual traditions to interact again.

Outside of the South Asian diaspora, Nusrat is best known due to his engagement with Peter Gabriel and the World music scene that propelled him on to the international stage.[37] This collaboration began in 1985 and resulted in NFAK gaining a wide non-Punjabi audience and arguably much greater recognition in the sub-continent. Some commentators have argued that Qawwali was a dying form, confined to the time of the *Urs/mela* and unattractive to younger audiences.[38] By receiving the endorsement of Peter Gabriel and as a corollary of a Western audience, this increased Qawwali's status thus enabling new audiences a potential to relate to the music. Whilst there is no doubt that NFAK drew on his international fame as a way of increasing exposure and prestige to the Qawwali form, he also maintained his engagement with the Punjabi diaspora. Indeed, his popularity with this audience maintained a significant impact on his musical innovation. This point is articulated in this 1993 interview on Zee TV:

> The new generation born in the UK, growing up here, they do not know what Heer Waris Shah is, who Sassi/Pannu are. These old, traditional things ... [such as Bulleh Shah's

poetry] ... to attract them to these things, I had an idea, which I mulled over for a long time about a certain type of experimentation. Those who like English, Western music, if we sing to them in our own way they won't be able to tolerate it. My experience has been to use western instruments with our classical style, the old tunes that are coming from the past, in Pahari or in Bhairvi, or other tunes that we could use in a new composition. In that way this would promote our culture ... and this was a new experience for me.[39]

What is critical here is the way in which Nusrat places himself in relation to what is perceived of as a 'lack' in the diasporic population often articulated in terms of religion. Given the way in which Qawaali is being marketed at the time in the World music market as 'spiritual', there would be a case for emphasising the religious aspect of the tradition. Yet this is not the argument put forward by Nusrat, rather it is those popular love stories, Heer Ranjah and Sohni Mahiwal, that transcend formal social boundaries of religion, sect and creed, which are chosen to engage with the diasporic audience. In one sense, these are the ideal texts to anchor Punjabis in a context where they are engaged in reformulating social relations in new settings and NFAK is keenly aware of this. In describing these new musical forms, he states:

This is a new form of music, I would not call this Qawaali, as that has its own basis and foundation, that is the art that we get from our elders and it is also our family art, we know what the requirements are for Qawaali and if you leave them then it is not Qawaali. We could call this an 'experience of sound', not Qawaali. The tradition of Qawaali is a complete thing and I would not say that an individual like me could change that. What I have done is bought in new rhythms. Looking at the atmosphere here, I saw what people wanted, what does the audience like to listen to ... [40]

In the volume *Dis-Orienting Rhythms* and subsequently the book, *A Postcolonial People* the argument that British South Asian popular music should be seen as a form in its own right, not derived solely from South Asia, but related to a number of transnational nodal points was put forward (Kaur and Kalra 1996; Ali, Kalra, and Sayyid 2006). NFAK in this interview, in a sense makes a similar point, not framed through the assertion of identity, but rather as central to a particular type of creative process, rooted in the Punjabi *qissa* tradition but routed through a mosaic of musical forms.

It is with this perspective that NFAK was able to transcend the divide between musical genres and the borders of political identity appealing to multiple audiences at several levels. His ecstatic reception in Bollywood in the mid-1990s led the way for many Pakistani artists to follow, with his nephew Rahat Fateh Ali Khan now almost entirely based in Mumbai. In the British context, NFAK crossed over from playing in Pubs and community centres into the emerging British Asian music scene of the late 1980s. My own encounter with his music came as part of the organising committee of the first National Festival of Asian Music held in Nottingham in August 1988. This open air event held over a weekend, heralded the beginning of the Asian *Melas* that are now a feature of the British summer.[41] NFAK performed a two hour set of his best-known Qawaalis, predominantly in Punjabi, enthralling the crowd of 5000 young people and families. Two years later, I was fortunate to see NFAK again, this time performing in a seated auditorium in Nottingham, to an invited audience. The sponsor of the event introduced the evening and also notified the audience that the evening would only consist of Persian language Qawaali. Whilst this may have come as a surprise to many of us sitting there, who had been bought up on NFAKs

Punjabi offerings, the performance was still mesmerising. This ability of NFAKs music to cross musical styles and performative spaces is perhaps best illustrated by my third anecdote. In 1991, the Paradise Club in East London hosted one of the first public Lesbian, Gay and Transgender South Asian nights. DJ Ritu played the latest Bhangra tracks and when *Kinna Sohna*, Nusrat's track, remixed by Bally Sagoo from the album *Magic Touch* was played; the floor was cleared by Naseer, a young man dressed in a flowing skirt (ghagra) and bindi on his forehead. He proceeded to dance to the track, *Kinha Sohna*, miming to dramatise the lyrics: *Kinna Sohna tainoon rab ne banaya, dil kare vekhda ravan (How beautiful God made you, I feel like spending all my time looking at you)* is a Punjabi track, with simple lyrics that come to life with the Latin rhythms that Bally Sagoo's remixing combine with the powerful vocals of NFAK. In each of these performance space, the *mela*, the auditorium and the nightclub NFAK's enduring appeal is in fore fronting the centrality of the creative process in his musical work where any narrow or closed sense of identity is abandoned.

Looking for *Punjabiyat*

The *Punjabiyat* that Nusrat's music evokes does not circulate in the realm of institutional and public politics, rather it reflects a process of becoming, a critical inception, rather than a fixed classification determined and maintained by the contours of the nation-state. This framing of *Punjabiyat* emerges outside of a social science/humanities discourse that is unable to cross the impervious Indo-Pak border or one that is solely focused on recovering or recreating a common culture. In Surjit Patar's poem, 'My Language is Dying', the lack of learning in the Punjabi language is contrasted with the economic and status requirements of learning English. The state and formal education system is dismissed as a possible saviour for the language, because for Patar, Punjabi was never something that king's or bureaucrats took kindly to, indeed, he lists the language's saviours as: 'Spiritual figures, poets, prophets, lovers, warriors, my people' (Shah 2004, 177). Indeed, despite NFAK's popularity, in the small academic literature on Qawwali he is ignored as being too commercial or too concerned with music to be considered a true Qawaal of the shrine. Perhaps this is because he fits better into the epithet of poet, lover or prophet, rather than authentic representative of an ancient tradition. The containers of Sufi music or Muslim culture that have gained currency in Western liberal circles are unable to hold the irrepressible energy of an NFAK singing: *Dha de Masjid, Bhan de Mandir* (Demolish the Mosque and break the Temple). Rather the focus is on those elements which resonate with a manageable and consumable commodity of religious music, regardless of whether it relates to a tradition or not. In this sense, NFAK's music like *Punjabiyat* remains on the margins of mainstream academic concern whether in India, Pakistan or the diaspora. This status of marginality, though, provides the concept with a critical edge which is enabling rather than paralysing and insightful rather than bland. Descriptors which apply equally well to the musical gifts that NFAK gave.

There are a few artists such as poet Surjit Patar and documentary film-maker Ajay Bhardwaj, who evoke *Punjabiyat* in a critical mode, but none as popular as NFAK. Ajay Bhardwaj's documentaries, filmed from 2003 onwards and based in East Punjab takes us into a deep exploration of the meaning of *Punjabiyat*.[42] In these films, a land-owner cries when reading about the partition, a woman devotee refuses to be filmed, a soldier of the Indian National Army describes his families shrine.

These characters are not presented as romantic figures resisting the overwhelming crushing forces of modernity, nor a comfort for those seeking nostalgia or refuge in the past. Rather, *Punjabiyat* emerges as the resilient space in which those wishing to express their humanity in the face of relentless degradation are able to speak. Hope arises in Bhardwaj's films in the music of those who perform at shrines across East Punjab, B.S. Balli Qawwal Paslewale, a group of musicians taking up the form only in the twenty-first century, a bagpipe player entirely concerned with his performance as a devotion to his pir and the examples go on. Bhardwaj alerts us to and is also subject to the charge of romanticism in the wake of the conceptualisation of *Punjabiyat* offered here. A critique that of all forms of identification no matter how conceived ultimately conceal and congeal other differences and in this context most notably that of gender and class/caste. Despite the taking of the female voice in many of the song texts (Abbas 2002), the universe of a critical *Punjabiyat* remains dominated by male performers. A video of a school girl singing Shiv Kumar Batalvi on the Facebook site, *Wasda Rahey Punjab*,[43] raises comments from the viewing public about the location of the girl in terms of being in India or Pakistan. The Facebook site, *Wasda Rahey Punjab*, is ostensibly targeted at those who can read the Shahmukhi script which is used to describe the group.[44] This gives rise to the assumption, as explored in the various comments, that the girl is singing in the courtyard of a school in West Punjab. This confusion is confounded by the generic nature of the girl's uniform, the common rural government class room setting and in fact the musical intonation and expression in the performance. Gender and class work in ways which play with the music listeners ability to neatly categorise and classify. A girl of this social class could still be in either a remote East or West Punjabi village, but once subjected to the scrutiny of those who can only see through the lens of the nation or religion *Punjabiyat* quickly disaggregates.[45] Rather it is the problematic of a girl singing or the impossibility of her living in a Muslim society that becomes the focus. Indeed, it is male voices that have been prominent in this article's narrative and Nusrat himself only drew one categorical boundary in his interviews and that was around the inappropriateness of women singing Qawwali.[46] *Punjabiyat* subverts one set of borders and asserts others and it is in the musical biography or NFAK that these processes are made most apparent.

Notes

1. Transcribed and translated by article author.
2. Taken from, recording on, NFAK, Vol. 8, 1985, Oriental Star Agencies (VHS). This particular couplet has been performed by many other artists most notably Sain Zahoor.
3. 5/3/13 BBC Radio 2: Guru of peace: An introduction to Nusrat Fateh Ali Khan, Nitin Sawhney.
4. NFAK has a single video with over 10 million hits, for example, whilst Fareed Ayaaz Qawwal's most popular is just over 800 K (Youtube November 2012). In personal communication with Mohammed Ayub, director of Oriental Star Agencies, he stated that NFAK still remains one of their best-selling artists.
5. According to Mohammed Ayub, Nusrat's first album recorded in 1973 featured the track 'Ni mai jana jogi de naal'.
6. Alternative sites might be sport (but this tends to be competitive in terms of national boundaries, i.e. India vs. Pakistan) or films (again these tend to be narrated within the frame of national competitiveness, such as *Dil bole Hadeepa*, though *Waris Shah – Ishq da Waaris* by Gurdas Maan is a notable exception) or even food (though issues of *halal* and *jhatka* again divide along religious lines).

7. It is also significant that formal musicological analysis is not included here though for those interested in this aspect, see Kalra (2014).
8. Prominent examples are the books: *Sikhs in Britain* by Tatla and Singh, *Salaam America* by Mohammed-Arif and *The Indian diaspora* by Jayaram, though there are numerous other examples.
9. This is despite the fact that diaspora researchers do not suffer from the problems that researchers based in India and Pakistan have in terms of obtaining visas to carry out research in each other's countries.
10. The volume *Sufism in Punjab* is dedicated to the memory of Nusrat and contains this epithet: 'Who stood as a bridge between West (Pakistani) Punjab and East (Indian) Punjab. Who emerged as the greatest cultural icon of the Punjabi diaspora that is spread in all continents of the world'.
11. Mostly, the role of West Punjab is completely ignored in Paksitani textbooks in favour of a national/religious combine. See Rosser (2004).
12. There are of course notable exceptions. The work of the Advanced Centre for Punjabi has been a remarkable contribution to the advancement of cross-border communication; however, this institute is primarily interested in technological innovation rather than studies of diaspora. For tools that can transliterate between Shahmukhi, Gurmukhi and Devanagri, see http://s2g.learnpunjabi.org/login.aspx
13. Though the distinction between heterodox Sufi and Allama Iqbal is tendentious and relates solely to the description of this period in the literature on Qawwali.
14. There are perhaps only three or four live recordings of Mubarak and Fateh Ali, most notably 'Naa Maar Naina De Teer' features Mubarak Ali and the young voice of Nusrat can also be heard. Accessed 8/11/2013. http://www.youtube.com/watch?v=gyQx_4gyREg&list=FLVhAUacNAu-vGN0B2UosLdg
15. Mateela Films, 1997. Accessed 2/4/2013. http://vimeo.com/8202106
16. Sakata played an instrumental role in organising a residency at the University of Washington ethnomusicology department for Nusrat.
17. For those not familiar with the texts of Qawwali, those that do not explicitly refer to the Prophet (and would therefore be called *naat*) are in their best form focus on love which is ambiguously positioned between the sacred and the secular (see Gunninder-Singh for examples).
18. All interviews are either in Urdu or Punjabi and translated by myself.
19. http://www.nusratfan.com/an-exclusive-interview-with-the-legend-nusrat-fateh-ali-khan/, 1989.
20. Nusrat Fateh Ali Khan, *The Last Prophet*, Jerome Missolz Film, 2003. http://www.youtube.com/watch?v=bl_iIr51uyGhw
21. Baud partially captures the meaning of word *Bazurgon* in the translation, 'saints'. But in an interview in the film the Last Prophet, NFAK used the word *bazurgon*, to refer to his father, uncles and other ancestors in the musical sense. It is those, who's footsteps Nusrat is following in.
22. Interviews conducted with five of the main Qawwal groups of Punjab; for more details, see Kalra (2014).
23. The video to the track 'Mera piya ghar aya' worked on an anti-Indian nationalism through the figure of the lost soldier.
24. Though there are notable internet groups such as Asiapeace and the work of many small organisations such as the Institute for Peace and Development in Lahore. See Purewal (2006).
25. The Pakistani Punjabi films *Kartar Singh* and *Maula Jat* are good examples of these caricatures.
26. This is based on general viewing of the channels PTV and QTV during 2008–2010 and then systematic analysis of three months of Qawwali programming on these channels in which (excluding live coverages of an *Urs*) there.
27. Like any cultural form, music can also be used to enhance and reinforce division. The use of music by the RSS and the burning of cassettes and CDs by the Taliban are cases in point.
28. Lok Virsa Institute, 1989.
29. Lok Virsa Interview, 1989.
30. The use of a Qawaali for a rape scene in the film *Natural Born Killers* takes place without Nusrat's knowledge as part of the generic selling and buying of music in Hollywood.

31. http://www.youtube.com/watch?v=_8srWWca_Uk&list=PL02C16C4815BEBF41
32. In certain Sufi poetry, the mehkhana, literally house of wine, is the place in which the devotee/lover drinks to replicate the intoxication of love.
33. *Hai Raj Dulara Mata Da* in OSA Vol. 8, Birmingham Video, 1985, performed in the Facroft Public House on Soho Road in Handsworth. See Koi boley Ram, Slough Gurdwara, OSA.
34. This was ultimately released as an audio CD by OSA in 1995 under the title Shabad Vol. 13, a youtube video of the event is available at http://www.youtube.com/watch?v=6rDpONbOL8U, accessed 7/1/13.
35. Accessed 3/3/1013. http://www.desiblitz.com/content/muhammad-ayub-founder-oriental-star-agencies
36. Accessed 17/1/2013. http://www.youtube.com/watch?v=V-EQecLSOcE&list=PL02C16C4815BEBF41
37. The idea of world music has been rightly critiqued in terms of musical exotica (Hutnyk 2000).
38. See http://www.nusratfan.com/an-exclusive-interview-with-the-legend-nusrat-fateh-ali-khan/, 1989.
39. Zee TV Interview. Accessed 9/1/2013. http://www.youtube.com/watch?v=PP7jJOfDlMQ
40. Zee TV Interview. Accessed 9/1/2013. http://www.youtube.com/watch?v=PP7jJOfDlMQ
41. Every major British city hosts an Asian mela with a formulaic combination of music, stalls and fun fair. These melas were initially funded by the state, but have increasingly become privatised. The BBC Asian network still funds a season of melas throughout the UK, see http://www.bbc.co.uk/asiannetwork/events/melas/2012/ for example. Religious groups have also started to hold melas, with the Birmingham Vaisakhi mela and Eid mela being particularly large. These events also involve marching around the city, providing an interesting perspective on the geography of diaspora in the inner city.
42. *Kitte Mil Ve Mahi* (Where the Twain Shall Meet), 2005; *Rabba Hun Kee Kariye* (Thus Departed Our Neighbours), 2007; *Milange Babey Ratan De Mele Te* (Let's Meet at Baba Ratan's Fair), 2012.
43. Accessed 3/4/2013. https://www.facebook.com/pages/Wasdaa-Rahay-Punjab/105165399647031
44. The English rendition of the group's aims is as follows. In this page, we try to highlight the beautiful punjabi culture, which is a soil of five rivers, we hope that you like our page and our posts, thanks for joining us, we belong to a punjab city, Mandi Burewala, Punjab, Pakistan.
45. Though the vast majority of the 1300 or so comments were complimentary and praising the child's voice rather than focusing on geographical location or religion.
46. Lok Virsa Interview, 1989.

References

Abbas, S. B. 2002. *The Female Voice in Sufi Ritual: Devotional Practices of Pakistan and India.* Austin: University of Texas Press.

Ali, N., V. S. Kalra, and S. Sayyid. 2006. *A Postcolonial People: South Asians in Britain.* London: Hurst.

Baud, Pierre-Alain. 1996. "Nusrat Fateh Ali Khan: le _qawwali_ au risque de la modernitée [Nusrat Fateh Ali Khan: the Qawwali and the risks of modernity]." *Cahiers de musiques traditionnelles* 9: 259–274.

Baud, P. 2008. *Nusrat Fateh Ali Khan: Le messager du qawwali.* Paris: Demi-Lune.

Cottle, Simon. 1994. "Stigmatizing Handsworth: Notes on Reporting Spoiled Space." *Critical Studies in Mass Communication* 11 (3): 231–256.
Dudrah, R. 2007. *Bhangra: Birmingham and Beyond*. Birmingham: Birmingham City Council.
Dudrah, R. 2010. "Haptic Urban Ethnoscapes: Representation, Diasporic Media and Urban Cultural Landscapes." *Journal of Media Practice* 11 (1): 31–46.
Frembgen, Jürgen Wasim. 2008. *Journey to God: Sufis and Dervishes in Islam*. Oxford: Oxford University Press.
Gill, Talwinder. 2013. "The Indian Workers' Association Coventry 1938–1990: Political and Social Action." *Journal of South Asian History and Culture* 4 (4): 554–573.
Hutnyk, J. 2000. *Critique of Exotica: Music, Politics and the Culture Industry*. London: Pluto.
Jacoviello, Stefano. 2011. "Nusrat Fateh Ali Khan: The Strange Destiny of a Singing Mystic. When Music Travels." *Semiotica* 183 (3): 319–341.
Kalra, V. 2014. *Sacred and Secular Musics: A Postcolonial Approach*. London: Continuum.
Kalra, V., R. Kaur, and J. Hutnyk. 2005. *Diaspora and Hybridity*. London: Sage.
Kalra, Virinder S., Umber Ibad, and Navtej K. Purewal. 2013. "Diasporic Shrines: Transnational Networks Linking South Asia through Pilgrimage and Welfare Development." In *Diaspora Engagement and Development in South Asia*, edited by Tan Tai Yong and Md Mizanur Rahman, 176–198. London: Palgrave.
Kaur, R., and V. Kalra. 1996. "New Paths for South Asian Identity and Musical Creativity." In *Dis-Orienting Rhythms: The Politics of the New Asian Dance Music*, edited by S. Sharma, A. Sharma, and J. Hutnyk, 217–231. London: Zed Books.
Malhotra, Anshu, and Farina Mir. 2012. "Punjab in History and Historiography." In *Punjab Reconsidered: History, Culture, and Practice*, edited by Anshu Malhotra and Farina Mir, xv–lviii. New Delhi: Oxford University Press.
Mandair, Arvind. 2009. *Religion and the Specter of the West: Sikhism, India, Postcoloniality, and the Politics of Translation*. New York: Columbia University Press.
Manuel, P. 2008. "North Indian Sufi Popular Music in the Age of Hindu and Muslim Fundamentalism." *Ethnomusicology* 52 (3): 378–400.
Mir, F. 2010. *The Social Space of Language: Vernacular Culture in British Colonial Punjab*. Berkeley: University of California Press.
Purewal, N. 2006. "Borderland Punjab." *Seminar*. http://www.india-seminar.com/
Qureshi, Regula.1986 [1995]. *Sufi music of India and Pakistan: Context and meaning in Qawwali*. Cambridge: Cambridge University Press.
Qureshi, Regula. 1992/1993. "Muslim Devotional: Popular Religious Music and Muslim Identity under British, Indian and Pakistani Hegemony." *Asian Music* 24 (12): 111–121.
Rosser, Y. C. 2004. "Contesting Historiographies in South Asia: The Islamization of Pakistani Social Studies Textbooks." In *Religious Fundamentalism in the Contemporary World*, edited by C. Saha, 265–307. Oxford: Lexington Books.
Roy, Anjali. 2010. *Bhangra Moves: From Ludhiana to London and Beyond*. Aldershot: Ashgate Publishing.
Rubi. 1992. Ahmed Aqeel Rubi, *Nusrat Fateh Ali Khan, a Living Legend*, translated from Urdu to English by Sajjad Haider Malik.
Sakata, H. L. 1994. "The Sacred and the Profane." *The World of Music* 36 (3): 86–99.
Shah, A. 2004. "Punjabi Poetry with English Translations." *Journal of Punjab Studies* 13 (1/2): 177–204.
Sharma, S., J. Hutnyk, and A. Sharma, 1996. *Dis-orienting Rhythms: Politics of the New Asian Dance Music*. London: Zed Books.
Singh, S., and I. Gaur. 2009. *Sufism in Punjab*. Delhi: Akaar Books.
Wimmer, A., and N. Glick Schiller. 2002. "Methodological Nationalism and Beyond: Nation-State Building, Migration and the Social Sciences." *Global Networks* 4 (2): 301–334.

Tracing Sufi influence in the works of contemporary Siraiki Poet, Riffat Abbas

Nukhbah Taj Langah

Department of English, Forman Christian College University, Lahore, Pakistan

This paper examines the work of nineteenth century Siraiki mystic poet Khawaja Ghulam Farid and traces his influence on a contemporary poet Riffat Abbas. I aim to shed light on the changing disposition of Siraiki poetry through content and textual analysis of selected *Kafis* written by both these poets. *Kafi* writing is observed as a discourse moulded to convey some political implications as it can be associated with the 'risky political times' as it challenges the theorocratic and religious institutions. I argue that while Riffat Abbas is inspired by Farid and claims to be his disciple, he does not aim to replicate his master work; his poems are resiliently abstracted because he compliments Siraiki nationalism more candidly as compared to Farid. Thus, his *Kafis* transform into critical manifestations of Abbas's own historical moment. I indicate how Abbas's work is important in the current historical context of this region and why the comparison between the two is important for a close understanding of Siraiki literary tradition and culture. This paper therefore presents a close reading of these traditional and modern *Kafis*, not only elaborating their spiritual meanings but also how the metaphors introduced in new *Kafis* speak to Siraiki nationalism and promise to enthral people belonging to Punjabi diaspora.

Introduction

This paper presents a meticulous scrutiny of the Sufi genre of *Kafi*, most popularly used in South Asian literature. My primary focus is on traditional and modern *Kafis* written in Siraiki language, largely spoken in South Punjab as well as in other provinces of Pakistan. *Kafi*, in South Punjab, is most closely identified with the mystic poet Khwaja Ghulam Farid (1845–1901), whose philosophy has strongly influenced established contemporary Siraiki poets such as, Riffat Abbas (dates). Farid was writing Sufi poetry around the period when American realism was at its peak (1865–1910) (Wright 1952; Spencer 1941). This is the time when Indian sub-continent was confronting colonization by the British and the history was in a transition phase for mystic poets. For all these reasons, Farid cannot be detached from the historical context which influenced him and the local population of this region which he aimed to represent by producing Siraiki *Kafis*.[1]

Kafi is a term derived from the Arabic word 'kaifia' and the Persian word 'kawafi' which means 'sufficient, satisfactory and amusing' (Langah 2011, 84–85).[2] While earlier attempts of writing *Kafis* constituted one or several couplets, Farid is known for extending the length of *Kafi* to multiple couplets. The musicality of this form is impossible to be translated into English; however, to some extent, this genre bears close resemblance with 'lyric' poetry in English. Some of the most significant features of this form include the use of concentrated Sufi philosophy combined with a rejection of self-imposed political institutions, introducing female narrative voice also epitomizing regional vernaculars representing peripheries (Burney Abbas 2007, 628). Within the political context of this region, the suffering female protagonist and roving minstrels in this form personify suffering of this land (Burney Abbas 2007, 625–626). Sufi poetry is still sung as a sign of political protest against illicit domination of certain institutions and classes (Burney 2002, 628). Farid's *Kafis* are popularly sung by most of the popular contemporary singers from Sindh and Siraiki speaking areas of Punjab provinces in Pakistan; including, Abida Parveen, Alan Faqir and Pathanay Khan.

In Siraiki literary tradition, this poetic form was predominant even before the popularity of Siraiki *Lok Geet* (folk song).[3] There is no set date establishing the exact emergence of *Kafi* within Siraiki folk tradition. However, its surfacing is traced through influence of Shah Hussain and Shah Latif's Sindhi poetry (Jampuri 1969). Khwaja Farid's writing style combines the themes of death, passionate worldly and spiritual love and grief associated with love. He wrote in various different languages including Punjabi, Urdu, Pashto, Sindhi, Hindi and Persian, but gained popularity mainly for writing in his mother language, Siraiki (Langah 2011). Like Bulleh Shah and Shah Abudul Latif Bhitai, Baba Farid Gunj Shakar (1175–1265) from Pakpattan, Shah Abdul Latif Bhitai (1689–1752) from Sindh and Khushal Khan Khattak from N.W.F.P (1613–1689), for Siraiki people and contemporary poets like Abbas, Farid epitomizes ethnic, linguistic and local culture.

Farid's Sufism embodies orality and folk culture of the Siraiki region intimately and the contemporary poets therefore feel consciously influenced by him as an icon of Siraiki identity. These poets therefore use *Kafi* form as a way of communicating with people using simple, local idiom. In order to disseminate Farid's Sufi ideology through this literary form and resist state pressures, Abbas and his contemporaries are being published in local literary journals such as *Jeevan Jog* produce self-published anthologies. Born in the ancient city of Multan, Abbas claims to master the *Kafi* tradition and argues that his 'The Revival of the *Kafi* Movement' initiated by him with other well-known contemporary Siraiki poets wish to save this classical form from dying (Langah 2011, 78).[4] For Abbas and his contemporaries, *Kafi* remains the only poetic form which simultaneously embodies, the poet's direct emotions, the philosophy of love, the expressions related to music and performance in local language and innate association with Farid's mysticism also reflecting in Siraiki *Geet* (folk song) like Urdu *Ghazal*. Like Farid, Siraiki language (*maa dharti*) and land (*maa boli*) both are strong identity markers for Abbas he uses folk symbolism, local images and topography of his motherland as the context of these *Kafis* (Langah 2011, 78).

Within the South Asian context, thus, *Kafi* is observed as representing and voicing the margins, resisting state pressures, promoting equality of genders, symbolizing and promoting vernacular folk culture and idiom or subtle promotion of faith related issues (Ali 1988, 81–94; Burney Abbas 2007, 627–628). While retaining these stances, this paper, on the one hand, focuses on the ways in which Abbas desires to follow Farid as a role model and a symbol of resistance against state pressures (Jampuri 1969, 128–267).

On the other hand, while struggling to revive Farid's *Kafi* form, he paradoxically reroutes from the traditional spirit of this mystic form and re-contextualizes it within the modern and shifting political landscapes of South Punjab. This two way pull, along with Abbas's intricate intentions of promoting Siriaki culture, results in a hybridized *Kafi*, which unpredictably receives decent acknowledgement by Siriaki readership. However, this paper argues that Abbas faces different kind of historical and political challenges as compared to Farid and therefore intentionally revives and reinvents this form with different realities in mind.

Since one of the focuses of this paper is exploration of the region of Punjab, it is significant to mention that Siriaki political activists propose the division of Punjab into two provinces, 'Central Punjab' and 'South Punjab', which includes twenty-three important districts of Punjab. In this context, their mother language and literature bear significant importance in terms of redefining the concepts of Punjab and Punjabiyat, which becomes challenging for the Punjabi community residing within Pakistan, India or those belonging to the Punjabi diaspora, who witnessed the traumatic event of 1947 partition and due to their ancestors separation or death during migrations now consciously identify with the history and culture of this region and cannot envision yet another bifurcation of Punjab.

Bearing this context in mind, this paper constitutes three main sections; the first section presents some examples and discussion on Farid's *Kafi* writing style and philosophy; the second section compares Farid's *Kafis* with Abbas's contemporary concerns reflecting through his contemporary *Kafis* and finally, the third section concludes this discussion by articulating the connection and disconnection between these traditional and modern *Kafis*.

Farid's mystic approach

Pantheist philosophy in Farid's **Kafis**

As indicated in the introduction, within Siraiki culture, *Kafi* is chiefly associated with Farid, his local mysticism and local language embedded within his motherland. This genre has traditionally been associated with spirituality and mystical strife of Sufi poets as also visible in the works of many Punjabi, Sindhi Sufi poets like Bulleh Shah, Sachal Sarmust and Waris Shah. Some critics contend that due to European colonization, Muslim Sufi scholars were inspired by the Western philosophy of 'pantheism' – meaning, god is everything and everything is god, which clearly reflects in the concept of 'Wahadat-ul-Wajood' in Khwaja Ghulam Farid's poetry (Haq 2003; Qaisar, 1998; Standford Encyclopedia of Philosophy, 2010).

To some extent, these mystics follow pantheist philosophy, according to which, there are six processes of God's creation. For pantheist Sufis, these stages are called *Sair-ul-Urooj* or upward march towards god. Following these stages of *tasawwuf* or mysticism, according to mystic philosophy, man passes through all these stages and reaches the stage of finding his true Self. This is when the journey towards god ends and results in a journey within god. These stages could further be elaborated as follows:

Fana-fi-Allah (The state of union with god when man loses his own idea of SELF)
↓
Baqa-bi-Allah (abiding by god or highest stage of human perfection)
↓
Sair Nazooli (Return to one's own self after full identification with the Divine Being as a perfect self now). (Haq 2003, 24–29)

Physical and spiritual love (Ishq-e-Haqiqi vs Ishq-e-Mujazi)

In order to illustrate similar spiritual connotations in Farid's mystic poetry, I will now discuss some stanzas from Farid's *Kafis*. Farid writes:

> With the name of Allah I uncovered my head and picked the burden of love.
> Ranjha[5] is mine, I am for him,[6]
> Such is written in the sacred book of fate,
> Right from the day of creation of the universe.
> O Fareed! separation has taken too long a period,
> I have almost burnt to ashes. Pity!!![7]

As indicated by many other critics and writers, there is a strong thematic similarity between the works produced by various Sufi poets, regardless of the language or cultural context in which they write. One example here is an illusion towards another Sufi poet, Waris Shah's (1722–1798) tragic legend of romance between Heer (from Jhang) and Ranjha (from a village near river Chenab) from Punjab. Heer and Ranjha's unrequited love never got accomplished due to their tribal rivalries and resulted in the suicide of these lovers.

This love story has both, physical and spiritual connotations. Farid, like many other Sufi poets in South Asian culture, conveys the theme of *Ishq-e-Mujazi* meaning, 'Love for a Beloved' as symbolized in his folk character, Heer's love for Ranjha and *Ishq-e-Haqiqi*, meaning 'Love for God' is a deeper or spiritual love of humans for God. The sense of oneness achieved through this *Kafi*, placed within the understanding of *Ishq-e-Haqiqi*, is ending the worldly desires and life and reaching the height of spirituality by uniting with God forever. Clearly, such connotations of love in Farid's poetry aim to achieve something which is beyond reality – love for God, which we are never sure is a reality or imagination. Paradoxically and in the physical sense, these lovers, as historical characters, challenge social hierarchies because both Heer and Ranjha embrace love to reject all the social differences that surround them.

In another *Kafi*, Farid writes:

> Allah is praised.
> Love's appearance is everywhere. (Haq 2003, 96)

And in another one,

> There is no difference between Ahad and Ahmed
> The essence and attributes are one.
> The 'Selves' of both are unique as well as their attributes are singular. (Haq 2003, 83)

In other words, an ideal (re)union with his true self is achieved by expressing oneness with his Creator and by dissolving the social differences between 'Ahad' and 'Ahmed'. This spiritual union with God can only be achieved when humans become capable of eradicating their worldly desires and dissolving social differences and this is what Farid aims to eventually achieve through his mystical strifet in these *Kafis*. In this context, the beloved or Ranjhan mentioned in Farid's poetry is in fact God as Farid's beloved and in his search for this beloved the poet wanders through the Rohi desert like Ranja's search for Heer. If analyzed from this angle of mysticism, for Farid, the reality is uniting with 'Ranjhan', or union with God.

(Call me not Heer, the beloved!) Now I have been transformed into Ranjha the lover; no difference has been left between him and me now. The fire of love has made me glow like itself. The pronouns 'you' and 'he' have melted away; only the pronoun 'I' is left over to be found in this entire universe. Only he who can find this great secret can succeed, and succeed in all trails. (Haq 2003, 86)

Paradoxes & ambiguities

In another *Kafi*, Farid writes,

> When I see the clouds floating on high and the rain drops trickling down in a light drizzle my eyes are filled with tears as a token of the remembrance of the dear one. The eyes become restlessly impatient for a face-to-face confrontation with the beloved and my arms flutter tremulously in the excitement of an amorous embrace. (Haq 2003, 57)

This excerpt depicts an idealistic picture of Farid's Sufi thought. The meaning within Faird's *Kafis* life is aimed much towards this search and the ultimate goal of uniting with 'a beloved', which is God. When the worldly existence loses meaning for him, he turns towards a search for his innermost self. While Farid aims to become an idealist and reformer of human condition by optimistically suggesting that the way to improve the human condition is spiritual pursuit and depth, realistically speaking, for a common man, this reunion might only be achievable through the reality of death (Claude 1981, 119).

Like this paradox of desiring to reunite with God and the impossibility of achieving this target (or achieving it only after death), there are several other paradoxes in Farid's *Kafis*. For instance, the paradox of Farid's choice of the real geographical location of the Rohi desert and his spiritual quest for God; one symbolizes a reality and the other symbolizes an imaginative search for someone who is beyond reality and even beyond worldly desires. Hence, there is a digression from daily chores performed by local people depicted in Farid's *Kafis* towards a spiritual quest, which is beyond these chores. In this context, Farid's *Kafis* are not just about spiritual association with God but also about Farid being realistically rooted in his mother culture and topography (his 'motherland'). In the discussion that follows, I focus on such aspects of Farid's *Kafis* which also create an inconsistency in his poetry by contradicting the idealist and romantic search for God in the form of a lover for a real pursuit of identity in his *Kafis*. In order to further emphasize his association with the Siraiki locale, he elaborates the routine activities associated with the 'local color' of the Rohi desert, 'seeking to portray faithfully the customs, speech, dress and living and working conditions of [his] locale' (Murfin and Ray 2009, 430). He also portrays the lower and middle class common characters from Rohi who are busy in daily chores. The daily chores in which these characters engage themselves represent the folk culture of this desert.

Various traditional references used by Farid sketch a realistic picture of an average woman living in the Rohi desert. These symbols relate to their daily activity of dressing up and looking presentable. For instance, *musag* is commonly used by people to clean teeth, *kajol* or eyeliner and colored herbs used to color lips are traditionally used as make-up in this region (All Poetry 2010). Similarly, a crackling crow is regarded as a symbol of a guest's arrival. Wandering through the Rohi desert, performing day-to-day activities and the ultimate goal of searching for a lover are the ideas constantly repeated in Farid's *Kafis*. This is the reality of Farid's life and Siraiki *vusaib* (land, culture and people) to which he belongs and wishes to realistically portray in his *Kafis* (Langah 2011, 61–96).

Comprehending Farid within current political context

A re-interpretation of Farid's *Kafis* within the contemporary socio-cultural and political context of Siraiki language and identity indicates another reality in Farid's *Kafis* – his origins as a Siraiki poet and his association with his motherland through his mother language, Siraiki, which somehow also transforms into an amalgamation of his spiritual association with the reality of his origins as a native poet (Burney Abbas 2002, 57). His resilient association with the Rohi desert, as a metaphor of his motherland keeps him deeply attached to both land and language (*Vusaib*), creating a link between his locality and poetic orality. Cholistan (Turkish word meaning, land of 'Chol' or sands) or Rohi refers to the desert areas of Bahawalpur from where this desert extends into India as the Thar. Thus, by depicting the topography and culture of Rohi, Farid remains entwined with the reality of his origins. In this context, Rohi becomes the nucleus from which surfaces Farid's themes of love, journey, quest, exploration, beauty and even mysticism in most of these *Kafis*. His desire for metaphysical realities therefore also hinges upon the material reality of this location. Through these *Kafis*, Farid therefore narrates his journey of understanding his own self and his identity, the Rohi desert plays a dominant role in the process of self-identification because it becomes a symbol of his motherland. His spiritual pursuit for a beloved through the barren, arid land of the Rohi desert, once again indicates his journey for finding himself (identity). Furthermore, he narrows down his focus towards the vivid details of Rohi's natural beauty, flora and fauna, which create a sense of harmony between his poetic inspiration and the natural beauty and conventional culture of Rohi (Malik 2000, 135–137).

On a mystical level, this desert becomes an important symbol in Farid's *Kafis* where, like most dervishes and Sufis, he seeks spirituality. It is a dual metaphor in Sufi tradition, symbolizing a place for finding peace and also a place of finding detachment from worldly affairs, as in the case of Farid who decides to choose an 'ascetic life' and 'hermetical strife' in the Rohi desert. The sheer wilderness of the desert accompanied by its barrenness creates a sense of peace for Farid who searches for God's presence in this wilderness. This desert inspires him to give up all his material interests, possessions and attractions in order to reach spiritual heights or, in other words, to unite with God. This search is further intensified through the mention of Farid's restlessness and lack of sleep in pursuit of his beloved or God. In some ways, he oscillates between the real (the Rohi desert) and the imagined (mysticism) pursuit of God but never gets over the conflict between the two. For him, this experience turns towards the multifarious experiences of love for the natural beauty of this desert, for a human beloved who is never found and finally, reaching God by giving up these physical pursuits. In the matured stage of his experience, everything symbolizes God and every path takes him towards God.

The female voices in Sufi poetry such as *Kafi* are particularly discussed by critics like Shemeem Burney Abbas. Burney suggests that sometimes such voices in Sufi poetry subdue the gender of Sufis and Dervishes and what becomes more important is the their spiritual ecstasy or state of mind, also regarded as *kefiat, zikr, fikr, lagan, khayal, qalaam, wijd* (Burney 18–19). The gender of the poet becomes irrelevant also because for God, this gender is irrelevant as long as the poet has faith in Him. Concurrently, the female voices used in *sufiana qalam* such as qawali also reflect 'submission to the master' (or God) (Burney 55).

In addition to his *Kafis*, where the female narrator awaits her beloved (God), the technique of using the female narrative voice is also followed in Farid's *Sejh* songs. Relating to the realistic aspects of Farid's poetry, these female voices can also be associated with Farid's efforts to depict the socio-cultural realities encapsulating the life of local women in his *Kafis*, as particularly reflected in his popular *Sejh* songs. *Sejh* is the bed lying in a bride's nuptial chamber which is sacred for her more than any other thing in her life. In Sufi poetry, a beloved waits near the *sejh*, awaiting to meet her beloved (God). However, Farid's parallel motif in such poems, just as in the *Kafis*, is also to portray the lives of ordinary illiterate and yet independent women who resist social pressures in a male-dominated society while keeping themselves busy in daily household chores like fetching water, looking after family and cattle or collecting cotton and *peeloons* (a seasonal and local fruit that grows in Rohi) (Haq 2003, 122). Farid feels inspired by these women and therefore wants to realistically capture their day-to-day activities in his poems, the jingling of their bangles and their desire to marry their lover by resisting the social and cultural pressures. These can all be read as realistic rather than mystic images in the poems.

My discussion so far indicates that Farid's *Kafis* have to be studied through this paradoxical real/imaginary or idealist/realist and real/mystic binaries. His *Kafis* cannot purely be studied under the heading of generic 'Sufi poetry' as this would mean detaching Farid from his realistic association with his mother language, mother culture and the topography of his motherland or Siraiki region. I have discussed elsewhere that Farid's political consciousness reflects through his resistance against the rule of British hegemony within the Princely State of Bahawalpur which integrated Farid's favorite haunt, the Rohi desert, again emphasizing his identity consciousness (Langah 2011, 31–60).[8] Associated with similar connotations in Farid's portrayal of Siraiki culture and regions is my understanding of Farid's realism theorized by Sarah F.D. Ansari's in her contention that Sufis become not only mediators between God and people but also between the rulers and the ruled, which further adds to the realistic aspects observed in Farid's *Kafis* discussed in this paper (Ansari 1992, 24–25).

Riffat Abbas's Contemporary *Kafi*

In the earlier discussion, I have indicated that Farid's clearly remains strongly rooted in his motherland symbolized through Rohi desert. The aim of his *Kafis* is also to represent the local culture of the region and preserve the legends and chronicles which are crucial parts of the folk and literary tradition. Hence, his notion of love whether understood from spiritual or physical angle also reflects his passion for his culture and his pride of being associated with it. This part of the paper focuses on Abbas's *Kafis*, bearing in mind that he aims to do the same but with different concern in mind and using different poetic puns.

Abbas and his anonymous 'friend'

> In the bowl of this world
> Look at the rose of our passion, my friend.
> Even if we do not eat together
> Even if we do not sit together
> We can at least dream together, my friend.
> Even if we do not drink together
> Even if we are strangers
> At least consider the color of our wine, my friend.
> The sun is setting on the lanes
> The river is almost at my door
> At least look at our restless hearts, my friend. (Abbas 2005, 7 and poetrytranslation.org)[9]

Abbas's *Kafi* quoted above indicates that the romantic images of physical love for a beloved combined with spiritual love for God, borrowed from Farid and other mystic poets, is overshadowed by the idea of ambiguous rejection by an anonymous 'friend' in Abbas's poem. The poet's repetitive emphasis on 'my friend' in every third line of all the four triplets almost transforms this character into the central character of the poem and someone who has made an impact on the poet's life. However, Abbas and his so-called 'friend' somehow remain detached perhaps on the basis of class, social or ideological difference in Abbas's *Kafi*. For the same reason, the poet is unable to even sit next to his friend to share a meal, drink or even enter into a dialogue. The theme of this *Kafi* presents an example of socialist realism when some kind of social or economic factor sets these friends apart. They represent two different classes or groups since it is usually 'economic forces [which] are real and have a profound effect on the distribution of wealth and power in the world, they always work in the context of the political struggle among groups and nations' (Gilpin 1984, 293–295). Abbas's 'friend' therefore remains a stranger (Stanza 3, Line 2) and clearly diverges from the mystical 'friend' observed earlier in Farid's *Kafis* with whom the mystic prepares to unite, both in the worldly and spiritual sense (Tahir 1988. *Qalam Khwaja Ghulam Farid*, 122–437). This friend may also be different from Rumi's (or other Pakistani mystic poets' such as Bulleh Shah's or Shah Latif's) idea of friend represented in their mystical poems but it is not the subject of this study to compare Abbas's *Kafis* with all these works. In other words, while Farid creates a 'spiritual twin' in the form of a human to whom the mystic poet remains spiritually attached or who becomes a reminder of the poet's association with God, Abbas's 'friend' strangely remains socially, ideologically and psychologically detached from him (Gilpin 1984, 293–295). Indeed, before reaching the stage of Farid's spiritual quest for his 'friend', a 'river' (Stanza 4, Line 2) of emotions forces Abbas to open his 'restless heart' (Stanza 4, Line 3) and initiate a dialogue with this friend through his poem. This dialogue clearly differs from Farid's efforts of writing *Kafis* as a dialogue between himself and God because Abbas somehow struggles to emphasize the left wing view of equality of classes.

Stream of consciousness

Similar ideas reflect through another *Kafi* as follows:

> Someone is coming
>
> From a distance any news can arrive
> The boat can reach its destination any time
> A river of thoughts is flowing
>
> Some form is emerging
> Something is happening
> Someone is silently smiling
>
> It can be a fresh fragrance
> Or a reeking smell
> A group is disembarking. (Abbas 2005, 12)

In literature, stream of consciousness refers to 'a narrative mode rendering an individual's subjective, ongoing, and often jumbled mental observation and commentary' (Murfin and Ray 2009, 487–488). Furthermore, stream of consciousness also refers to 'the mental flow of one or more characters, a flow determined by free association rather than logic or linguistic rules (e.g., of pronunciation or syntax)' (Murfin and Ray 2009, 487–488). The 'river of thoughts' is a perfect example of his stream of consciousness as he goes on to create a free association between 'a boat', a 'river of thoughts', 'someone silently smiling', a 'fresh fragrance' or a 'reeking smell' and a 'group disembarking' (Abbas 2005, 12). The poet's mind follows a stream of consciousness by making references to the past and present through his conscious mind. It is significant to note the way Abbas complicates the imagery and symbolism and leaves it to the reader to unpack their intricacies. The poem nostalgically revives the memory of someone who is or was perhaps in a relationship with the poet as he associates the boat with this person's arrival and as a metaphor of hope.

A political group?

Entwined with this psychological exploration is the political concern reflecting through Abbas's expression here. Unlike Farid's *Kafis*, the readers are forced to explore the connotations of the group that he mentions in the last line. He discusses two different classes/groups to which the poet and his friend belong as indicated in the first *Kafi*. The poet seems to be in a tranquil mood and yet waiting for someone's arrival or some expectation. Like the first *Kafi*, an anonymous friend who is neither a beloved nor God, as in Farid's *Kafis*, further complicates his expression and its interpretation. There are no strange forms emerging in Farid's poetry as in these examples of Abbas's works. Abbas unintentionally changes the understanding of the traditional *Kafi*; a hope for change for his 'group' becomes his major interest in both the examples quoted above. This group almost turns into a representative and reminder of human beings as being part of often competing groups instead of discrete individuals. Such groups may also be interpreted as nation-states, tribes, city-states, kingdoms or empires (Abbas 2005, 12). With such a mention of a group also emerges the idea of nationalism, which is somehow related to the poet's loyalty and association with his group, and which repeatedly appears in his *Kafis*.

In this context, my reading of Abbas's *Kafi* indicates that this group might also be representing the Siraiki people struggling to reinforce their cultural or ethno-linguistic identity in Pakistan. In some ways, as a political realist, Abbas contemplates the notion that, 'all these more noble goals will be lost unless one makes provision for one's security in the power struggle among social groups' (Abbas 2005, 12). Clearly, no such complexities are implied in Farid's *Kafis*, as discussed in the previous section of this paper. As compared to Farid's *Kafis*, Abbas's ideas appear abstract and incoherent, intentionally created to give a peculiar character to these modern *Kafis* written with the intention of conveying something different as compared the Sufi message in Farid's *Kafis*.

Abbas's apprehensions

Another characteristic feature of Abbas's *Kafis* is a sense of insecurity which is not part of Farid's traditional *Kafis* discussed earlier.

> In which juncture do we stand?
> So many eyes are watching
>
> ....my eyes and forehead
> My entire face is drained out
> The rain drops are watching us

> We sat to eat
> Or to converse
> We are being watched closely
>
> How long will we stay together?
> Will we always be running or sitting?
> The geese are persistently watching us. (Abbas 2005, 13)

In this *Kafi*, Abbas seems to find himself at a complicated juncture in his life and remains disturbed because he faces the paranoia and anxiety of being 'watched' closely, not by God but by the anonymous eyes of the people that he does not trust. For this reason, he is in a state of conflict and has lost the power to decide which path to choose in his life. The poem seems to focus on the theme of lovers/friend under surveillance, whether he sits together with his friends to eat or converse. He feels insecure about breaking the unity of his assemblage as people or even nature is watching them. The most disturbing symbol in this poem is that of the geese as they stand between the poet and his beloved, making noises and disturbing their interaction. The beauty and noise create a paradox is his *Kafis* – a paradox which never reflects through Farid's works.

The city of Multan

Another interesting characteristic of Abbas's poetry is that he moves away from Farid's preferred symbol of the Rohi desert and robustly associates with his native and historic city of Multan, which still remains the political and cultural center of Siraiki region. Thus, the setting of Abbas's *Kafis* becomes more urbanized as compared to Farid. As a matter of fact, instead of substituting Farid's topographic location of Rohi, Abbas seems to connect the cultural and geographic magnitude of Rohi (previously part of the Princely State of Bahawalpur) with the political standing of contemporary capital Multan. The idea bears political connotations too because the present demand for Siraiki province has been absurdly moulded into a demand for two provinces named Bahawalpur–Janoobi Punjab as this would mean the domination of Punjabi identity can be maintained through Mohajir/Punjabi dominated minority in majority of South Punjab. Despite the fact that the bill for a new province was passed in the last (Pakistan Peoples' Party) government, the current regime (Pakistan Mulsim League, Nawaz Group commencing it tenure in Spring 2013) has rejected the idea of new provinces mainly due to the fear of losing its self-imposed authority over the province of Punjab and disregarding the other provinces resisting this authority. It is therefore impossible to overlook the political connotations of the City of Multan in the works of contemporary Siraiki writers like Abbas.

> One mosque, one date tree
> A blue sky in the background
>
> The world of my heart is enlivened
> Reached Multan in the evening
> With a red sky in the background
>
> Eyes cried at night
> Strange smile
> With a red sky in the background
>
> In which season did the geese fly?

A red sky in the form
A red sky in the background. (Abbas 2005, 29)

Here, Abbas regards the city of Multan as his final destination in this *Kafi*. However, unlike peace and harmony that Farid finds in Rohi, there is a peculiar disturbance associated with this city; the natural color of its sky turns from blue to red as the poet artistically paints its picture while reaching this destination. The mention of red color distressingly signifies multifarious meaning; for instance, passion, blood, death, heat and sunset, strangely overwhelms the reader. As readers, we are left wondering why such a disturbance is associated with this city, including the repetition of the metaphor of geese migrating, presumably signifying, winter, death, lost hope for the poet or even his fellow natives migrating from their mother land (Siraiki region) in pursuit of work, resources or a better life.

Revision of Sufi imagery

Convoys of sunshine have arrived
In the bazaar of our city

Some grape juices are flowing
Some scents are emerging
Some fragrances in rows

Look at the eatables
Look at the drinks
The weather itself is intoxicated

People are coming to watch
Western winds are blowing
Watch them. (Abbas 2005, 10–11)

Seeking after God is a process accomplished through worldly friendships, being intoxicated with the wine or passion for God's love are all distinctive feature of Farid's *Kafis*. The mention of wine in his *Kafis* mainly symbolizes the height of emotional and spiritual experience which is fulfilled after uniting with God. This is often compared to being drunk with wine as a metaphor for spiritual ecstasy. It is significant to note that the use of wine as a symbol of intoxication with love for God is replaced by a more realistic image of grapes in Abbas's *Kafi*, which also associates the poem with the sensuality of a *ghazal* form of poetry usually written in Urdu. In this *Kafi*, Abbas repeatedly mentions the fragrances of this city, the most important one being the scent of grapes which intoxicates the environment and people. However, here the directness of Abbas's use of grape juice in relation to the 'bazaar of his city', somehow conveys only a literal meaning of becoming intoxicated, not by spiritual love but just for the sake of finding relaxation, perhaps to escape from the daily socio-political traumas that surround his city and overwhelm the poet. Like the noises of geese mentioned earlier, there is a sense of disturbance in the poet's city – there seem to be multiple voices emerging from some kind of activity and movement going on in his city and shattering its peace and tranquility along with poets flow of thoughts. The readers are informed that these noises are an outcome of the arrival of a convoy, or a gathering of his friends, or as a result of their discussions, which reverts back to my earlier idea of Abbas representing a group. These people are in a constant state of dialogue or communication. However, the cause of this agitation or the political connotations of this commotion are never candidly addressed by the poet.

> The voices are rising
> In our silent city
>
> Some sounds of spring
> Some jingling voices of monsoon
> A fair of delight
>
> Some call for dialogue
> Arrival of a convoy of love
> A moment of sharing secrets
>
> Old voices
> Old sayings
> Secrets revealed through open doors. (Abbas 2005, 15)

Like earlier *Kafis*, here, the poet is hopeful, even joyful, again mentioning arrival, but also nostalgically harking back to history represented through the old voices like Farid's.

Traditional vs. Contemporary *Kafis*

In the first and second sections of this paper, I have argued that both Farid and Abbas use *Kafi* as a way of epitomizing their folk, ethnic, cultural, psychological and political realities depicted through the 'gravity, and the physicality of objects', geographical locations which keep them rooted in their mother culture; land and language as representatives of this culture (Lebowitz 1942, 359 and 429). A comparison of traditional and contemporary *Kafi* writing style stretching over a period of one century indicates that despite Abbas's claim of being an ardent disciple of Farid, he somehow remains distracted, presumably because he is recontextualizing Siraiki *Kafi* from a postcolonial perspective and feels exposed to various political pressures that surround him.

Despite his claim of being a Sufi poet, the deviation from Sufi philosophy becomes discernible in case of Abbas and is significantly connected with the depiction of social and political realities more strongly as compared to Farid. Consequently, as compared to Farid, Abbas's *Kafis* can be analyzed through this connection with Siraiki nationalism and divergence from Farid's traditional mystic approach. A comparison of Farid's and Abbas's *Kafi* writing style indicates that as a matter of fact, Abbas finds Farid's Sufi thought as a source inspiration but probelmatizes it by introducing social or political themes in his own *Kafis*. His claim that he is following Farid's *Kafi* writing style, themes and aims at reviving therefore becomes contentious. Hence, while Abbas regards himself as the initiator of 'The *Kafi* Movement', he paradoxically diverges from Farid's theme and style and uses *Kafi* to resist the pressures of those literary circles who challenge his modern movement as a symbol of damaging Farid's tradition and image.[10]

Through this discussion, I contend that unlike Farid, who typically fuses romanticism and naturalism with mysticism, Abbas moves a step forward by obfuscating these images and reframing them within the socio-political context of the Siraiki region. Consequently, we observe several disturbing, metaphors and symbolism in his *Kafi* which reflect his shift from Farid's traditional themes and writing style. Abbas therefore reiterates his own themes, style and complicates the imagery to the extent of shifting from *Kafi* to free verse (*azad nazm* in Urdu) related to his political context and real experiences and yet desires to regard this kind of poetry as *Kafi* (Basit Bhatti, N. Langah, 25 August 2013). In other words, Abbas reformulates *Kafi* and gives a modern touch to it. Bearing the postcolonial conditions, experiences and audience in mind, Abbas consciously and effectively transforms *Kafi* and its 'Sufi' stance more strongly into realistic and political representation of Siraiki language, culture, identity and most importantly, nationalism.

For instance, it becomes problematical to assess the ambiguous nature of love in Abbas's *Kafis* as compared to Farid. Farid's *Kafis* clearly focus on shifting from worldly love towards love for God and spirituality. Hence, the most significant border in Farid's *Kafis* is between the physical and spiritual worlds, which the poet overcomes by passionately praising his Creator and feeling one with him. Whereas, the sense of love in Abbas's works evokes the feeling of the poet being disturbed about another group, friend or an individual and there he gets caught up in these worldly affairs more effectively as compared to Faird. Abbas aims to bridge the tangible gap between himself and the strangely distant 'friend' who seems to be turning into a foe. This friend can be interpreted as a political friend too. While Abbas denies his standing as a resistance poet, paradoxically, his *Kafis* can be read as gesturing towards postcolonial binaries of 'us' and 'them', which, are usually imperceptible in Farid's *Kafis* or generally refer to man and God.[11] The kind of binaries with which Abbas is engaged can at some level be interpreted as possibly his inadvertent diversion from Farid's traditional style of writing.

Stylistically, Abbas diverges from Farid's *Kafi* too and does not follow the traditional rhyme patterns and stanza style fastidiously. Thematically, he modifies these *Kafis* as he has more obscure social and political concerns as compared to Farid. As a matter of fact, he also shifts from the traditional setting, themes and folk symbolism (like *peelo*) found in Farid's *Kafis* and Rohi desert is intentionally replaced by the political center and capital city of Multan (FNas also in case of Ansari). Correspondingly, the natural beauty and tranquility of Rohi is replaced by the urban ambiance and commotion due to the evolving socio-political changes that the poet experiences in this city. Furthermore, the disconcerting journeys that the poet and his friends experience and their mysterious convoys commence and end in the city of Multan. In this process of rerouting himself, Abbas's *Kafis* can be critiqued for losing the traditional musicality and folk imagery that Farid has always tried to preserve in each and every *Kafi* that he wrote. As a matter of fact, Abbas's complicates the imagery and gives it the shape of a modern *nazm* (poem) diverting from the genre of a *Kafi*.[12]

Since Abbas's comparison with Farid is done within the context of evolving political awareness within the Siriaki speaking region, it is significant to discuss the relationship between political activists and creative writers belonging to this region. Since 1970s, when the Siriaki political movement focusing on the demand for the creation of Siraiki province through the bifurcation of Punjab surfaced, there has been a lot of debate about Siraiki activists and creative writers joining hands. It is a historical fact that initially Siraiki political movement was inspired by and initiated through Siraiki literary activities like *Jashn-e- Farid* and literary conferences in the 1970s (Langah 2011, 23–27). Currently, however, both argue that their work represents Siraiki culture and identity, there is a clear contemplation over the divergence between the roles of a political activist as compared to that of a creative writers writing in Siriaki. Unlike many South Asian, South African and African writers like Faiz Ahmed Faiz, Ngugi Wa Thiongo and Dennis Brutus who have ardently acknowledged their political role and have also paid a price for it, majority of Siraiki writers and intellectuals today have tried to disassociate themselves from critical political activism, sometimes due to state pressures or in response to their conflict with the political leadership or in order to underline the preeminence of literature over politics. Presently, as also indicated through my discussion in this paper, both the political activists and writers tend to fight for the same cause – their political recognition – but they seem to fork their fronts as follows: literary and political. Abbas's argument that he is not producing resistance poetry is based along the same lines.[13]

This paper has identified Abbas's diversion from tradition Faridi style as a form of resistance that he develops when he writes under the political pressures of the society in which he operates or he intentionally avoids to acknowledge his work as resistance poetry. Consequently, Abbas improvises traditional Siraiki *Kafi* transform into a convoluted hybrid of Farid's poetic form and contemporary *Kafi*. I have argued that there is a conflict between his effort to keep Farid's name and genre alive and his political concerns that make him write such poems, which he regards as *Kafis*. At a political level, this resistance might also be emerging out of the ideological differences between Siraiki and non-Siraiki identities or the distance between Siriaki activists and writers while Abbas resists these pressures by emphasizing and re-emphasizing the significance of *Kafi* poetry as both, a folk and political expression within Siraiki culture. It is significant to note, however, that like political activists who use Farid's couplets as slogans, Abbas is using Farid's *Kafis* as a symbol of Siraiki culture and identity, which in fact transforms into a kind of political activism too.

A comparison between Farid and Abbas's *Kafis* also indicates that this divergence might be a postcolonial necessity where Abbas finds himself under intense socio-political and cultural pressure, and in such a historical moment that he is compelled to address different concerns from those of Farid. Abbas justifies this divergence by proposing that the *Kafi* needs to be redefined and reinterpreted within the changing political contexts. Diverting from the relationship between God and man, Abbas, truns towards the internal and external conflicts that surround him and the readers of his *Kafis*. While Abbas resists the fact that his *Kafis* should be included in the list of poetry which is being regarded as an expression of political resistance, this paper indicates that his 'The Revival of the *Kafi* Movement' can also be associated with the earlier literary movements and political movements emerging in Multan in the postcolonial era. In this context, 'The *Kafi* Movement' can be interpreted as a movement which, more than reviving Farid's folk tradition and mysticism, aims to present *Kafi* as a symbol of preserving Siraiki cultural identity and hence turns into a symbol of resistance. A classic example of this resistance and his political concerns about non-Siraiki speakers dominating this city reflect through this *Kafi*:

A new ruler is in the city
He cannot speak the language of this city

People are busy
in their daily chores
A new ruler is in the city

Eyes convey some messages
Intellectuals interact with him
A new ruler is in the city

The officer was summoned initially
Then the rest

A new ruler is in the city

A cold pond
Some grains in the room
A new ruler is in the city

Then a carriage visits through the city
The flowers dried on the paths
A new ruler is in the city. (Abbas 2005, 43–44)

Finally, as mentioned earlier in this paper, the emergence, awareness and reinforcement of Siraiki identity have turned into a challenge for the people belonging to Punjabi diaspora as, 'The region was repeatedly subjected to annexation, partition and reorganisation' (Singh 2012, 153). The Punjabis across the borders strongly associate themselves linguistically, culturally and religiously (Singh 2012, 153). Siraiki political question, often interpreted as a political gimmick by the Punjab government and Pakistani establishment, in fact, is a postcolonial phenomenon and has turned into a threat to the globality of the Punjabi identity across the borders of Indian Punjab, Pakistani Punjab and the diasporic Punjab (Singh 2012, 154).[14] It is therefore hard for them to imagine that a new identity, such as Siraiki, can assert its political claim over a certain territory by proposing yet another bifurcation of Pakistani Punjab, which once again means, 'renegotiating identity' for Punjabis (Singh 2012, 163). While reinforcing language as an important identity marker for them, within Pakistan, disregarding Siraiki language and literature is an important part to play in this tension and my paper has aimed at assessing Abbas's work as an important resistance tactic employed by Siriaki writers.

Notes

1. For my comprehensive discussion about the association between Farid's mystic poetry and Siraiki culture, see Langah (2011, 31–60).
2. I have briefly discussed Farid's Kafis and Abbas's efforts of reviving the genre of Kafi here.
3. Riffat Abbas in conversation with author, 2010.
4. Riffat Abbas and Shamim Arif, Multan in conversation with the author, 25 August 2004.
5. The beloved is traditionally Heer in these *Kafis*.
6. Here, the name of Ranjha is used metaphorically for the beloved (or God).
7. http://oldpoetry.com/opoem/61221-Khwaja-Ghulam-Farid–R-A—Kafi-18–with-english-translation-first [accessed 16 August 2010].
8. The desert is most significantly located in the ex-Princely State of Bahawalpur. In the early 1970s, there was a movement demanding the revival of this Princely state. However, later, the initiators of this movement acknowledged the demand for a Siraiki province due to the close linguistic, ideological, cultural and ethnic affiliation between Bahawalpur and Multan. In the recent years, the establishment floated the idea of the creation of Bahawalpur Province to weaken the territorial, economic and political strength of the demand for a Siraiki province. For a detailed discussion on this subject, see Langah (2011, 18–20).
9. This is my translation of the *Kafi* quoted above. For the original version, see this translation is also published on the official website for Poetry Translation Centre (UK). www.poetrytranslation.org [accessed 6 September 2007]. For Punjabi *Kafi*, see Petievich (2007, 9–11 and 33–43). This book discusses *Kafi* poetry as a Punjabi poetic form without any mention of this form being popularly used in Siraiki language.
10. Riffat Abbas and Shemeem Arif in conversation with author, 2009.
11. Riffat Abbas and Shemeem Arif in conversation with author, 2009.
12. Basit Bhatti (contemporary Siraiki prose writer) in conversation with the author, August 2013.
13. This argument is based on my personal observations as a political activist and my engagement with Siraiki nationalists, activists, intellectuals and writers.

14. However, such a post-Partition or diasporic association amongt the Siriaki community is yet to develop and strengthen at transnational level and then be made as part of an academic discourse and theorizing of Siriaki culture and identity.

References

Abbas, Riffat. 2005. *Ishq Allah Saen Jagya*. Multan: Kitab Nagar.
Ali, S. Asani. 1988. "Sufi Poetry in the Folk Tradition of Indo-Pakistan." *Religion & Literature* 20 (1): 81–94.
All Poetry. Accessed August 16, 2010. Available from: http://oldpoetry.com/opoem/61221-Khwaja-Ghulam-Farid--R-A---Kafi-18--with-english-translation-first
Ansari, F. D. Sarah. 1992. *Sufi Saints and State Power: The Pirs of Sind, 1843–1947*. Cambridge: Cambridge University Press.
Burney Abbas, S. 2002. *The Female Voice in Sufi Ritual*. Austin, TX: University of Texas Press.
Burney Abbas, S. 2007. "Risky Knowledge in Risky Times: Political Discourses of *Qawwali* and *Sufiana-kalam* in Pakistan-Indian Sufism." *The Muslim World* 97 (4): 626–639.
Claude, Inis L. 1981. "Political Realism Revisited." *International Studies Quarterly* 25 (2): 198–200.
Gilpin, Robert G. 1984. "The Richness of the Tradition of Political Realism." *International Organization* 38 (2): 287–304.
Haq, Mehr Abdul. 2003. *Visions of Khwaja Farid: Past & Present*. Multan: Siraiki Adbi Board.
Jampuri, Kaifi. 1969. *Siraiki Shairi*. Multan: Bazm-e-Saqafat.
Langah, Nukhbah Taj. 2011. *Poetry as Resistance: Islam & Ethnicity in Postcolonial Pakistan*. New Delhi: Routledge.
Lebowitz, Martin. 1942. "Concerning Realism in Literature." *The Journal of Philosophy* 39 (13): 356–359.
Malik, Ameer Hafiz. 2000. *Selected Kafis of Khwaja Farid*. Multan: Siraiki Adbi Board.
Murfin, Ross, and Supriya M. Ray. 2009. *The Bedford Glossary of Critical and Literary Terms*. New York: Palgrave Macmillan.
Petievich, Carla. 2007. *When Men Speak as Women: Vocal Masquerade in Indo-Muslim Poetry*. New Delhi: Oxford University Press.
Poetry Translation Centre. Accessed September 6, 2007. www.poetrytranslation.org
Qaisar, Shahzad. 1998. *Dimensions of Khwaja Farid's Metaphysics*. Multan: Siraiki Adbi Board.
Singh, Pritam. 2012. "Globalisation and Punjabi Identity: Resistance, Relocation and Reinvention (Yet Again!)." *Journal of Punjab Studies* 19 (2): 153–172.
Spencer, T. Benjamin. 1941. "The New Realism and a National Literature." *PMLA* 56 (4).
Stanford Encyclopedia of Philosophy. Accessed November 9, 2010. http://plato.stanford.edu/entries/pantheism/
Tahir, Siddique, ed. 1988. *Kalam Khawaj Farid*. Rahim Yar Khan: Khwaja Ghulam Faird Book Foundation.
Wright, Quincy. 1952. "Review: Realism and Idealism in International Politics." *World Politics* 5 (1): 116–128.

Exiled in its own land: Diasporification of Punjabi in Punjab

Abbas Zaidi

School of the Arts and Media, University of New South Wales, Sydney, Australia

Diasporic studies are about groups of people living as exiles, self-exiles, migrants and immigrants. Suppression of diasporic communities in various forms in their former (but original) homeland and/or adopted homeland has been the major concern of diasporic studies. Issues such as language, culture, identity and religion form core areas of these studies. Recently, the peripheral existence of various minorities within a country/society has led to diasporic studies in which no transborder situation is involved, which shows that the scope of diaspora as a discipline or research field has widened a great deal. However, there is one aspect of diasporic studies which has remained almost unexplored on its own. This is what can be termed as non-people issues facing diasporic fates of their own. Language, culture and religion can be such issues. This paper takes up the status of the Punjabi language in the state of Punjab in Pakistan. It claims that Punjabi language is being exiled from various domains of society by no other agent or institution but the Punjabis themselves. In other words, the Punjabi language is facing 'dispersion' at the hands of its own (native) speakers. Adapting a well-known sociolinguistic model called the Ethnolinguistic Vitality Model, the paper seeks to document the diasporic status of Punjabi language in Punjab. The findings of this paper belie the generally made claim that the power of a language is related to the power of its speakers. Despite being the language of the overwhelming majority group of Punjab and Pakistan, Punjabi is alien in its own homeland.

Introduction

Diaspora, or *a* diaspora, is about migration, displacement, or dispersal. At its simplest, the term can be understood as an international phenomenon whereby dispersal or migration takes a group of people from one country or region to another. Thus, it has been claimed that a diaspora is a group of people 'of a common national origin or of common belief living in exile' or 'people of one country dispersed into other countries' (Choi 2003, 10). In its classic formulation, the scholars of diaspora do not understand it in synchronic terms; a diaspora is fundamentally a diachronic phenomenon involving more than one generation. A diaspora is a group of people who (have) migrated and 'their descendants who maintain a connection to their homeland' (Plaza and Ratha 2011, 3). In modern times, the concept of diaspora is not tied down to physical displacement/dispersal. Today, even a total lack of physical displacement can be interpreted in diasporic terms whereby a group identifies itself based upon its particular affiliations, inclinations and interests while staying in its 'homeland' (see Brubaker 2005, for details). A diaspora in this sense is a community symbolically constructed by people which is a 'resource and repository of meaning and a referent of their identity' (Cohen 1985, 118).

A diaspora, then, is about humans. That nonhuman issues and phenomena are not studied on their own in diasporic terms is because these are considered ancillary to humans and their situations. For instance, and relevant to this paper, languages of diasporic communities are treated in terms of minority and/or multicultural issues. The major part of research on language attrition or shift taking place in diasporic communities is about how a majority language backed by the majoritarian state apparatus, such as language planning, undermines a community (minority) language (Tollefson 1991; Phillipson 1992; Skutnabb-Kangas and Phillipson 1994; De Varennes 1996). The same is true of indigenous/native languages which have faced discrimination at the hands of exophoric or formerly colonial but now local rulers who happen to be in majority too.[1] It is rare that a language is treated as an agent *per se* and studied as such. It is even rarer that a language is treated as an agent on its own facing a diasporic situation (dispersion/displacement), especially a language which is the overwhelming majority language of a country and suffers at the hands of its own speakers.

This paper proposes to extend the debate on language/linguistic rights into natural, even human, rights by understanding Punjabi language (hereafter Punjabi) in the province of Punjab in Pakistan as an independent identity and report if its rights are being violated or not. This proposal may sound like a plea for linguistic anthropomorphism (which is certainly not), and a question may be raised if a language can be treated on its own terms. The answer is in the affirmative. Just like a river can be taken on its own,[2] a language can also be understood as distinct from its users, especially when the very users/speakers of it have been pushing it into obsolescence.

The thesis of this paper can be formulated thus: *despite being Pakistan's overwhelmingly majority language and having no threat from another language or ethnolinguistic group, Punjabi is facing diasporification within its own homeland.*

The Punjabi language in Punjab

Punjabi is the majority language of Pakistan. The province[3] of Punjab is Pakistan's largest political-administrative unit whose population is more than 60% of the country's population. Punjabis are not just the most numerical group in Pakistan, they are also the most powerful ethnolinguistic entity in the country. If in the national assembly (i.e. the parliament) a party wins all the seats from Punjab,[4] it will form a comfortable majority to rule Pakistan because Punjab's seats exceed those of all the provinces and administrative regions of Pakistan combined. Details from the latest census of Pakistan, which was held in 1998,[5] are given in Table 1.

The above figures speak for the dominance of Punjabi on the linguistic cartography of Pakistan. The population of the Punjabis within the province of Punjab is well over 80%.[6]

Methodology

As indicated above, the diasporification of Punjabi is about its extreme marginalization. Marginalization of a language is related to what in sociolinguistics is known as

Table 1. The Census of Pakistan 1998: language distribution.

Language	Speakers (%)
Punjabi	44.15[a]
Pashto	15.42
Sindhi	14.10
Seraiki	10.53
Urdu	7.57
Baluchi	3.57
Others	4.66

Source: Census of Pakistan-1991 (1998).
[a]Mohiuddin (2007, 26) claims that the population of the Punjabis is '48%.

language health, language vitality, language attrition and language obsolescence. These issues are part of a subfield of sociolinguistics known as *Language Maintenance and Language Shift* (LMLS), or *Language Shift* (LS). Thus, a well-known LMLS/LS model called the Ethnolinguistic Vitality Model is employed in this paper to find out if Punjabi is undergoing a process of diasporification in Punjab.

The reason for selecting the Ethnolinguistic Vitality Model (hence, the EVM) is that a number of sociolinguists have successfully used it in order to find out the state of viability and vitality of the languages of their various foci (Giles and Rosenthal 1985; Cenoz and Valencia 1993; Currie and Hogg 1994; Mann 2000; Sayahi 2005). The following section will examine the EVM with reference to this paper. It will also be pointed out why this model is important for this paper.

Ethnolinguistic vitality model

In 1977, Giles, Richard, and Taylor (1977) presented the EVM, which they believed could point to the sustainability of a language. According to them, ethnolinguistic vitality of a group

> is that which makes a group likely to behave as a distinctive and active collective entity in inter-group situations. From this, it is argued that ethnolinguistic minorities that have little or no group vitality would eventually cease to exist as distinctive groups. Conversely, the more vitality a linguistic group has, the more likely it will survive and thrive as a collective entity in an inter-group context. (Giles, Richard, and Taylor 1977, 308)

The EVM parameters of an ethnolinguistic group can be summarized thus: (i) status (economic, social and sociohistorical); (ii) demography (distribution of the group in the national territory, its number, proportion and concentration and (iii) institutional support (formal such as mass media, education, government services and informal such as industry, religion and culture.

The economic status, according to Giles et al. (1977, 310), is 'the degree of control a language group has gained over the economic life of its nation, region or community'. Baker (1993), commenting on the economic status, says that where a minority language community experiences considerable unemployment or widespread low income, the pressure may be to shift to majority language.

It has been observed that an economically dominant class is able to manipulate other classes (Taylor 1993; Pieter 2001). This is done through different means such as media, education and cultural practices. It is usually the case that the economically dominant classes are the ruling classes in their respective polities. It is their values which become national values, and it is their icons, which become national icons (Boggs 1984; Duong 2002). One of the repercussions of economic domination can be linguistic domination of an economically dominant group's language over other languages in a given scenario and it usually serves as the *lingua franca* (Bisseret 1979; Adler 1980). Korth's (2005, 146) research backs this argument thus:

> The acceptance of Russian as superior language consequently led to the negation or rejection of Kyrgyz language and culture. In order to fit into society's norm and to be accepted many Kyrgyz children before independence claimed to be Russian.

In the maintenance of a language,[7] *social status* and *sociohistorical status* are two important factors and are closely related. People whose language has a low social status or who themselves have a low view of it are likely to shift to another language. On the other hand, a socially high status language is more likely to be maintained. If a language is supposed to have played a significant part in the past, it can still have symbolic value for its speakers in the present. Regarding *social status* and *sociohistorical status* with reference to *language status*, Giles, Richard, and Taylor (1977, 312) argue, '... history, prestige and the degree of standardization may be a source of pride or shame'.

The demographic parameter refers to the geographical distribution of a linguistic group. Migration and emigration affect viability of a language. If members of a language community are scattered in different locations, a shift might well be on its way; but if after moving out from their provenance they settle down as a (linguistic) group in the host community, there is no reason why they cannot maintain their language. Li's (1982) study of Chinese Americans supports this view: The Chinese living in Chinatowns have maintained their language compared with the Chinese living elsewhere in the United States. Similarly, Clyne (1982) found that in Australia, those ethnic Maltese who were living close-by as a community were able to maintain the Maltese language.

Institutional support should be interpreted in terms of power in its various institutional manifestations. Take the media, for instance. The media can undermine minority groups just by ignoring them (Wilson and Gutierrez 1985). If a minority's language and culture are excluded from the mainstream media, its prestige and prospects are likely to suffer (Siapera 2010). Reading (1999) chronicles Scottish and Welsh campaigns in the nineteenth and twentieth centuries when these two languages did not find much place in the mainstream (English) media. In these campaigns, 'linguistic rights and minority language mass media' were closely bound up (Reading 1999, 179). Speakers of minority languages in Zimbabwe, especially those belonging to the districts of Beitbridge, Binga and Plumtree, have long expressed their frustration with the little coverage given to their languages on TV. Since these languages are excluded from the mainstream media, their speakers 'feel excluded from mainstream Zimbabwe society in the sense that they are forced to endure information blackout in their own languages' (Ndhlovu 2009, 158). Dei and Shahjahan (2008, 58) give the example of Ghana where non-Akan languages are considered 'minority tongues which are often excluded by the mainstream media, schools and learning centers'.

If a minority group carries out its religious activities in its own language, it will likely be maintained for a long time given the emotive significance of religion. Religious activities, medium of instruction and the employment world are some of the greatest factors supporting and strengthening a language's vitality. We may conclude that the EVM tries to give a wide-ranging account of the factors behind a language's vitality.

Ethnolinguistic vitality model: A critical view

The EVM has been criticized for various reasons. One of the earliest criticisms was made by Husband and Khan (1982) who faulted it for being statistically inadmissible; they argued that instead of being based on ethnic groups, the model should have been based on language communities. Thus, they called it 'an uncritical naming of parts' (Husband and Khan 1982, 195). Dornyei has criticized the EVM for its 'oversimplification of interrelationship of ethnolinguistic groups' (Dornyei cited by McKenzie 2010, 35). Currie and Hogg (1994) in their research on Vietnamese refugees in Australia found that the EVM needed modifications. They argued that the EVM should be understood in terms of language vitality, political and economic vitality and cultural and religious vitality. Landry and Allard (1994) reconceived the EVM in terms of four capitals: demographic, political, economic and cultural.

Perhaps the most incisive critique of the EVM has come from Williams (1992, 206) who argues that the model is based upon a 'contradiction' which is evident all over. The contradiction is that although the model is subjective, Giles, Richard, and Taylor (1977) relate it to objective social factors. Giles et al. refer a group's vitality to its esteem of its own language. But, according to Williams, if status evaluation is based upon a group's own culturally conditioned values, then the out-group's esteem 'derives from a different set of values' (Williams 1992, 208). Williams thinks that the EVM is unsatisfactory in its claim regarding the degree of control a group exercises over economic resources because it conflates control of economic resources with 'group coherence or enclosure' (1992, 208). Another problem which Williams encounters in the model is that it does not deal with two significant dimensions of inequality: gender and social class. Besides, there is little regarding the struggle that a minority wages for its rights.

Despite its limitations, the EVM can be a good indicator of a language's vitality. For instance, institutional support given to a language, that is, its teaching in schools, can greatly increase its vitality at the cost of other languages. Thus, sociolinguists in general have found the EVM productive. Schweigkofler (2000, 63), for example, thinks that the EVM is a 'good starting point' to understand a language's 'capacity for progress'. Meyerhoff has called it 'reliable' (2006, 108). Saxena (1995) acknowledged its usefulness in his study of the Punjabis of Southall in England. Singh (2001) in his study of multilingualism in India, and Rasinger (2007) in his study of Bengali in East London also found the EVM useful.

As has been reported above, the EVM has been used by a number of sociolinguists to assess the heath, vitality, etc., of various languages of their focus. But it cannot be used indiscriminately. Its explanatory power can adequately be utilized only when it is adapted to the needs of a given situation.

In the discussion on the diasporification of Punjabi in Punjab below, various parameters of the EVM discussed above have been adapted into *postulates* followed by *responses* to postulates (their confirmation or refutation) and *elaborations*.

Diasporification of Punjabi in Punjab

Based upon the postulates derived from the EVM, this section will discuss whether or not Punjabi has been undergoing diasporification in Punjab. The postulates cover all three areas of the EVM: status, demography and institutional support.

Status

Postulate 1: The Punjabis as an ethnolinguistic group face unemployment and fall in the low-income group in Punjab.
Response: No; the Punjabis are in no way at a disadvantage in terms of employment or low income compared with other groups.
Elaboration: Punjabis dominate not just the province of Punjab, but the entire country of Pakistan. From the very establishment of Pakistan in 1947, the Punjabis have been, in Alvi's words, the 'most privileged group' (1986, 25). He elaborates his point thus:

> The Punjabis were preponderant in the bureaucracy and the army and held key positions in the state. They became visible as the new dominant group, winning out over other regional groups who had less than their due share of education, jobs, and power. (Alvi 1986, 25)

Postulate 2. As an ethnolinguistic group, the Punjabis' contemporary as well historical social status has been lower than other ethnolinguistic groups in Punjab.
Response: No; historically Punjabis have either ruled Punjab or have been under the rule of foreigners (e.g. the Moguls and the British). The entire subcontinent has been under foreign rule in the past. Within their own province, i.e. Punjab, the Punjabis were the eyes and arms of the foreign occupiers and were never relegated to the lower socioeconomic position. In the present times, the social status of the Punjabis is the highest not only in Punjab but also in entire Pakistan.
Elaboration: Historically, the Punjabis have dominated their own province. Before the British colonizers defeated Maharaja Dalip Singh in 1848 and annexed Punjab, it was exclusively the Punjabis who had been ruling Punjab for some time (Chopra 2003). The Sikh rule of Punjab did not exclude the Punjabi Muslims; the latter acted in the highest bureaucratic and military positions. The British rule did not suppress the Punjabis. On the contrary, they were co-opted by the British to become the most significant part of their military might. According to Singh,

> Punjab was one of the last provinces in India to become a part of the British empire in India and, therefore, remained under British rule for a shorter time than most other regions in India. Far-reaching and rapid economic, political, social and cultural changes took place in Punjab during British rule. A large number of Sikhs and Muslims from the peasant communities became soldiers in the British army; canal irrigation networks were developed in some regions of Punjab; the landed elites of all the three main religious communities [i.e., Hindu, Muslim, and Sikh] cooperated with each other in seeking mutually beneficial arrangements by collaborating with the British authorities. (2008, 54)

Later, when the British introduced democracy in India, it was the Punjabis who formed their own government comprising the representatives of the three Punjabi communities, viz., Hindus, Muslims and Sikhs. Interestingly, since the Punjabi Muslims were in majority in Punjab, the chief minister of the province was always a Muslim.

As noted above and will be noted below too, since the creation of Pakistan, the Punjabis have dominated the country. Thus, the Punjabis face no inferiority complex in terms of their contemporary or historical social status.

Postulate 3. Overall, Punjabis are politically and economically a poor group.
Response: No, economically and politically, the Punjabis are the most powerful ethnolinguistic group in Pakistan.
Elaboration: A number of research studies can be cited to support the point that the Punjabis dominate not just the province of Punjab but the entire country of Pakistan in economic and political terms. For instance, Banuazizi and Myron (1986, 4) say, 'In Pakistan, the Punjabis ... are the politically dominate group within the bureaucracy and the military'. Levinson (1998, 268) makes the same point when he says that it is the Punjabis who 'dominate the government and military, the two most powerful institutions in Pakistani society'. Adeney (2009, 119) has observed that,

> The size of the Punjab, reflected in its electoral dominance, means that national political parties have to win in the Punjab if they wish to form a national government. Political parties that articulate regionalist agenda are either consigned to a small number of seats in their respective provinces or cannot gain the support of the Punjab for their regionalist agendas as these agendas normally have anti-Punjab hue.

A Pakistan scholar has this to say,

> Punjabi domination in Pakistan is so conspicuous that many non-Punjabis consider Pakistan to be an imperial state, the state machinery of which is monopolized by a dominant ethnic group at the expense of the other ethnic groups. (Shah 1997, 141)

Demography

Postulate 1. The Punjabis are a minority ethnolinguistic group in Punjab. Their population is scattered in Punjab which makes them an incoherent ethnolinguistic group.
Response: No; the Punjabis are the majority ethnolinguistic group not only in Pakistan but in Punjab also. We have seen the proportion of the Punjabis in Pakistan's population. In their own province, their population is exceedingly higher than any other group. West (2009) in her study of the peoples of Asia and Oceania says that over 90% of the population of the Punjab is comprised of Punjabis.
Elaboration: In such a situation, it would not be possible even to visualize, let alone content, that the Punjabis are a minority or scattered group in Punjab.

Postulate 3. Migration and/or immigration has affected the Punjabi population of Punjab in a significant way.
Response: The Punjabis migrate to foreign countries. Karachi in the province of Sindh has a significant Punjabi population. But the migration has not affected the population of Punjab at all.
Elaboration: With around 90 million Punjabis living in Punjab, migration or immigration is not an issue in the percent case.

Postulate 4. Interethnic marriages have affected the Punjabis as an ethnolinguistic group.
Response: No such pattern has ever been documented.

Elaboration: Qadeer in his study of ethnicity in Pakistan has found that although ethnic isolation is an uncommon phenomenon, interethnic marriages is not common at all. To quote him,

> There is no part of the country that has been left untouched by the flow of people of diverse ethnicities. . . . . . The only area in which ethnicity, rather more precisely tribal or *biradri* ties, remains largely unbreached is in matters of marriage and family. Interethnic marriages are rare, except in districts of historically co-inhabiting ethnic communities of Balochis and Sindhis. (Qadeer 2006, 76)

Postulate 5. The Punjabis birth rate is low compared with other ethnolinguistic group.
Response: The population growth of the Punjabis is no less than that of any other ethnolinguistic group.
Elaboration: Pakistan's census and studies on birth rate have never documented any dwindling of the Punjabis. The Punjabi population has always been overwhelmingly dominant.

Institutional support

Postulate 1. The media are heavily owned by non-Punjabis. Thus, Punjabi language and culture do not find enough exposure.
Response: The media, both in its print and electronic form are overwhelmingly controlled by the Punjabis.
Elaboration: Pakistan's top media houses, both print and electronic, such as Jang/Geo, Waqt and Dunia are owned by Punjabis. There is no way non-Punjabis can undermine Punjabi language and culture.[8]

Postulate 2. In various government institutions and especially policy-makers are non-Punjabis who do not make pro-Punjabi language policies (e.g. language planning).
Response: All government institutions are controlled by the Punjabis.
Elaboration: As has been documented above, the Punjabis control Pakistan economically and politically. In terms of government, governance and policy-making, the Punjabi control is complete and unchallenged. This fact is repeatedly noted by scholars such as Mohiuddin (2007) and Alvi (2011). In Alvi's words,

> In Pakistan. . . the dominance of a single salariat group, Punjabis, in the military and the bureaucracy has given rise to an authoritarian political system even during periods when there was a semblance of representative 'democracy'. (2011, 90)

The same point is made by Wilson too,

> Punjab has historically determined Pakistan's destiny since 1947. It has supported and sustained authoritarian regimes and has greatly influenced the ouster of unpopular governments. (2009, xix)

Postulate 3. Religious activities are carried out in Punjabi.
Response: Not at all; Urdu is the language of religious activities in Punjab. Punjabi is not supposed to be fit for religious activities.
Elaboration: The Punjabis do not use Punjabi for religious activities. They practice diglossia, which is a sociolinguistic situation (Fishman 1970; Wardhaugh 1986) in

which one language performs higher functions (called the H language) and the other performs lower functions (called the L language). According to Wardhaugh,

> A key defining characteristic of diglossia is that the two varieties are kept quite apart functionally. One is used in one set of circumstances and the other in an entirely different set. (1986, 88)

The Punjabis have set aside their own language as the L language and Urdu the H language when it comes to performing religious functions. Those who have dared to offer prayers in Punjabi have been even manhandled (Malik and Salim 2004). Every research study carried out in this respect has verified this claim (Mansoor 1993; Rahman 1996, 2002; Zaidi 2013).

Postulate 4. Punjabi is taught in schools.
Response: Punjabi is not taught in Punjab at any level.
Elaboration: Sindhi and Pashto are taught in schools in their respective provinces (Sindh and Khyber-Pakhtoonkhwa) where they are compulsory. But Punjabi is not taught in any school in Punjab. It is interesting to note that Punjabi can be taken as an optional subject in colleges. At the university level, one can do Master's or PhD degrees in Punjabi, but when it comes to teaching Punjabi in schools, the Punjabis themselves have chosen not to do so.

Postulate 5. Official correspondence in Punjab can be carried out in Punjabi.
Response: Not at all; it is Urdu and English which are the languages of official communication in Punjab.
Elaboration: The reasons are more or less the same as given in response to the preceding two postulates.

Postulate 6. Punjabi can be used on a political forum such as the Punjab assembly.
Response: Never; Punjabi has officially been banished from significant official political forums such as the provincial legislative assembly.
Elaboration: The Punjabis themselves have banned the use of Punjabi on a forum like the Punjab legislative assembly. In the rest of the provinces in Pakistan, elected legislators take the oath of office in their own languages (Sindhi, Pashto, Balochi, Urdu and Kashmiri), but in the Punjab assembly, it is forbidden to do so, and those legislators elect who wanted to take the oath in Punjabi were warned of disqualification by the speaker of the assembly (for details, see Zaidi 2010).

Postulate 7. There is an official or unofficial academy which promotes Punjabi.
Response: There are official institutions like the Punjabi Adaby [i.e. Literary] Board, but it is practically dysfunctional.
Elaboration: When a language is banned or discouraged at every official and nonofficial level, academies are meaningless. The academies established to 'promote' Punjabi are meant to act as places where rulers can 'adjust' their cronies.

Discussion

'Language shift' says Romaine (2012, 320), 'involves a *loss* of speakers and *domains* of use, both of which are critical for survival of a language'. There is an absolute consensus among sociolinguists on it (Gal 1979; Fasold 1984; Fishman 1991; Dorian 1992). The question arises: What can possibly make a sociopolitically and numerically overwhelming and secure group exile its own language from various domains? Or more specifically: Why have the Punjabis of Punjab, the ruling elite of Punjab as well as Pakistan, exiled their own language from various domains?

Different scholars have identified a number of factors which play a part in the marginalization or obsolescence of a language. For example, Weinreich (1974 [1953]) recounts the following factors: age, geography, group membership, indigenousness, occupation, rural/urban residence, sex and social status. Other factors which have been studied are migration, industrialization, urbanization, language prestige and the medium of instruction (e.g. Dorian 1980; Edwards 1985). Romaine (1995) recounts that factors which play a great part in language shift are: status of language, attitudes of a language's speakers, the role of school, language policy, speakers' inability to maintain their language in the home domain and insufficient learning of a language by the younger generation. According to Gal (1979), the factors that cause language shift are: industrialization, urbanization, loss of isolation, loss of national self-consciousness and loss of group loyalty. Fasold (1984) enumerates several factors for language shift such as migration, industrialization, school language, urbanization, language prestige and the composition (small or big) of population. Kulick (1992) claims that migration, industrialization, urbanization, proletariatization and government language polices determine if a language will undergo a shift or not.

None of the above factor answers the question about the Punjabi language. I would like to focus on one cause behind the diasporification of Punjabi: the language attitude of Punjabis. 'In the life history of a language', argues Baker, 'attitude may be crucial. In language growth or decay, restoration or destruction, attitudes may be central' (1988, 112). Gardner (1985) and Holmes and Harlow (1991) share Baker's view. Gardner (1985) considers attitudes as components of motivation and thinks that the preference for speakers' choice of a language, dialect or accent is influenced by their attitudes.

Punjabi is undergoing diasporification because of the attitudes of the Punjabis. This claim is supported by major works done on the sociolinguistics of Punjabi in Punjab/Pakistan. It has been reported that the Punjabis view their language as 'vulgar' and consider it to be fit only for jokes and mockery (Mansoor 1993; Rahman 1996, 2002; Schiffman and Spooner 2011; Zaidi 2013). The next question is: Why do the Punjabis have negative attitudes toward their own language? The answer to this question can be given in postcolonial terms.

According to the official narrative, Pakistan was created in the name of Islam. In order to foreground Pakistan's Islamic credentials, the ruling elites made everything local/indigenous suspect. On the contrary, everything which had some Arabic connection, however minimal or bogus, was given legitimacy and authenticity. Irfani offers a very powerful argument. He writes that since 1947, the time when Pakistan was established, there has been a steady ascent of an 'Arabist shift'. He defines this shift as the tendency to view the present in terms of an imagined Arab past with the Arabs as the only 'real/pure' Muslims, and then using this 'trope of purity for exorcizing an 'unIslamic' present. Consequently, the Arabist shift lost the eclecticism and intellectuality that were the basis of a creative South Asian Muslim identity, and this has led to a hardening in the understanding of Islam as a result of imagining Pakistanis in Arabist terms' (Irfani 2004, 148). He goes on to say,

The Arabist shift touched new heights through a convergence of General Zia-ul Haq's politically motivated Islamization of Pakistani state and society and the U.S.-sponsored *jihad* in Afghanistan on the one hand, and the fallout of the Iranian revolution, the Kashmir dispute, and uneven development on the other. Such a convergence was also boosted by romantic notions of an Arab-centric popular imagination as indeed the ground realities of multiple economic interests. For example, in a romanticized notion of Pakistan's breakup in 1971, the secession of Bangladesh is seen as a consequence of the failure to adopt Arabic as a national language; whereas cooperation in defense-related areas at the level of the state has been augmented by joint Pak-Arab business ventures that include partnership by "political" families, such as the family of the former prime minister Nawaz Sharif. There has also been a huge increase in the remittances of Pakistani expatriates from the oil-rich Arab states. Moreover, the Arabist shift is also underscored by the fascination of many Pakistanis and especially the religio-political groups with Talibanic Islam—generally seen as a slide toward a tribal, anti-intellectual and misogynist view of Islam promoted by a narrow interpretation of the Quran. And although the Taliban is not Arab, Talibanic Islam is a vigorous manifestation of the Arabist shift, of which Osama bin Laden has become the icon par excellence in Pakistan today. (Irfani 2004, 148–149)

Eric Cyprian, a well-known Punjabi and one of the leaders of the pro-Punjabi movement from the 1960s to the 1990s, also argued that the reason the Punjabi language was pushed to the margin by the ruling elite of the country was because of the past of the Punjabis and the Punjabi language. According to him, from the earliest times, foreign invaders had to pass through Punjab to attack Delhi, the capital of India. The Punjabis resisted all of them whether they were Muslim or non-Muslim. Thus, resistance to the foreign invaders became a part of the Punjabi culture, and the Punjabi poetry chronicles at length the bravery of the Punjabis against the foreigners. Hence, the foreigners, Muslim or non-Muslim, understood very well the political power of the Punjabi language and did everything to denigrate it, especially the British who brought Urdu-speaking administrative and police officers from Uttar Pradesh in order to consolidate their hold on the province of Punjab and its residents (Cyprian 1991).

The Punjabis' attitudes toward Punjabi can be understood from a socioeconomic or the so-called Marxist, angle too. The Punjabis are the dominant ethnolinguistic group in

Table 2. Fishman's GIDS.[a]

Stage 8	Social isolation of the few remaining speakers of the minority language. Need to record the language for later possible reconstruction
Stage 7	Minority language used by older and not younger generation. Need to multiply the language in younger generation
Stage 6	Minority language is passed on from generation to generation and used in the community (e.g. provision of minority nursery schools)
Stage 5	Literacy in the minority languages. Need to support literacy movements in the minority language, particularly when there is no government support
Stage 4	Formal, compulsory education available in the minority language. May need to be financially supported by the minority language community
Stage 3	Use of minority language in less specialized work areas involving interaction with majority language speakers
Stage 2	Lower government services and mass media available in the minority language
Stage 1	Some use of minority language available in higher education, central government and national media

[a]This table is Baker's adaptation (Baker 1993, 58).

Pakistan. By denigrating their own language, they have denigrated all the indigenous languages of Pakistan. Urdu is not indigenous to Pakistan; it is the language of those Urdu-speaking people who migrated to Pakistan after Partition. Urdu used to be identified with Muslims and Islam in pre-Partition India (as opposed to Hindi/Hinduism). After the creation of Pakistan, Urdu was declared the national language of Pakistan and stood (stands) for Islam and the Islamic identity of Pakistan. Thus, by embracing Urdu at the cost of Punjabi, the Punjabis have monopolized the national-Islamic language which has helped them in perpetuating their hold on the rest of the ethnolinguistic groups of Pakistan. Hence, Urdu is an ideological weapon in the hands of the Punjabis, the dominant group in Pakistan.[9]

Conclusion

This paper began with the thesis that the Punjabi language is undergoing a process of diasporification at the hands of its own speakers and in own homeland. The ethnolinguistic model adapted to understand the process has helped understand this process. However, just like any other theory or model, the EVM is not the only instrument to gauge the societal state of affairs of a language. The diasporification of Punjabi language in Punjab is so pervasive and so much taken-for-granted that it is not an issue among its speakers. One may type 'advertising/advertisements in Lahore' or 'graffiti in Lahore' into the 'Google image' dialogue box and find out that not a single text will appear in Punjabi; the only languages are (mainly) Urdu and (to some extent) English. This is evidence of the indifference and insensitivity on the part of the sparkers of Punjabi themselves.

Now that it is obvious that Punjabi is undergoing a process of diasporification, the matter can be dealt with from two angles: First, let Punjabi's process of diasporification continue where it meets its seemingly inevitable fate and second, ponder ways to stem the process of diasporification. For the latter, Fishman (1991, 87) has come up with what he calls a 'graded typology of threatened statuses'. He has developed the Graded Intergenerational Disruption Scale (GIDS) which he likens to the Richter Scale. GIDS in Fishman's own words 'may be thought of as a sociocultural reverse analog to the sociopsychological language vitality measures that several investigators have recently proposed' (1991, 87). GIDS has eight stages (Table 2):

In sociolinguistics terms, Punjabi will be taken as a minority language given its status in Punjab. All the GIDS stages, with the exception of Stage 8, can be exploited to benefit Punjabi. But that is possible only when a community in question is willing to see its language prosper and functional in various domains. But in the present case, the first angle seems more relevant because the Punjabi themselves are driving it into obsolescence.

When speakers of a language consider it vulgar, its future is bound to be defined by functional recession. This is what has been happening with Punjabi. It is on account of the attitudes of the Punjabis that Punjabi has no value, worth or utility. In societal terms, Punjabi's domains are too few to guarantee its viability; it is more of liability than asset. Thus, in its own homeland and among its on speakers, Punjabi is an alien.

The present paper has focused on the objective, macro aspect of the diasporification of Punjabi. There is immense scope to do research work on subjective and micro aspects of the diasporification of Punjabi. For instance, using methods like ethnography and phenomenology, people's relations with Punjabi can be explored in terms of language use, language repertoire and language attitudes. The use of Punjabi at work place and between social classes is another area where the claim of its diasporification can be verified.

Notes
1. Some of the examples are Australia, Canada, New Zealand and the USA.
2. As reported in *The New Zealand Herald*, in August 2012, a New Zealand court conferred a legal entity on the Whanganui River. A spokesman for the Minister of Treaty Negotiations announced, 'The Whanganui River will be recognized as a person when it comes to the law in the same way a company is, which will give it rights and interests'. The agreement was signed on behalf of Whanganui Iwi by Brendan Puketapu of the Whanganui River Maori Trust, which represents a group of Iwi along the river, and the Crown in Parliament. For details, see Shuttleworth (2012).
3. The equivalent term for 'province' in India or the United States is 'state'.
4. The province is referred to as 'Punjab' or 'the Punjab'. In this paper, the definite article is dropped.
5. The census of Pakistan which was supposed to be held in 1991 was actually held in 1998. After that, the latest census was supposed to be held in 2008, but given the country's volatile situation, it has not been held so far. For details, see Zaidi (2010).
6. Interestingly, some scholars may claim that the percentage of the speakers of Punjabi is not as low as 44.15 as shown on the table but 54.68%: Seraiki is a dialect of Punjabi, but it has been separated from Punjabi on the political basis. Rahman (1996 and 2002) has pointed out that Seraiki as a separate language was the result of the movement in the 1960s which sought to redress economic deprivations suffered by the people of South Punjab, the so-called Seraiki belt. Some scholars of Seraiki contend that Seraiki and Punjabi are not different languages but two varieties (Nadiem 2005; Shackle 2007). This is, however, a controversial issue and involves political economic and emotional issues. This also involves sociolinguistic issues like what constitutes a language/dialect and who decides what a language/dialect is and what basis. This is why, I have avoided this matter because it cannot be mentioned in passing.
7. Language vitality is an area within LMLS. Maintenance or shift of a language depends on its vitality.
8. I have had years of experience as a journalist in Pakistan.
9. This aspect needs to be explored in greater details.

References

Adeney, Katherine. 2009. "Democracy and Federalism in Pakistan." In *Federalism in Asia*, edited by B. He Brian Galligan and Takashi Inoguchi, 101–123. Cheltenham: Edward Elgar Publishing.

Adler, Max K. 1980. *Marxist Linguistic Theory and Communist Practice: A Sociolinguistic Study*. Hamburg: Buske Verlag.

Alvi, Hamza. 1986. "Ethnicity, Muslim Society, and Pakistan Ideology." In *Islamic Reassertion in Pakistan: The Application of Islamic Laws in a Modern State*, edited by Anita M. Weiss, 21–48. Syracuse, NY: Syracuse University Press.

Alvi, Hamza. 2011. "Politics of Ethnicity in India and Pakistan." In *Perspectives on Modern South Asia: A Reader in Culture, History, and Representation*, edited by Kamala Visweswaran, 87–99. Oxford: John Wiley & Sons.

Baker, Colin. 1988. *Key Issues in Bilingualism and Bilingual Education*. Clevedon: Multilingual Matters.

Baker, Colin. 1993. *Foundations of Bilingual Education and Bilingualism*. Clevedon: Multilingual Matters.

Banuazizi, Ali, and Weiner Myron. 1986. "Introduction." In *The State, Religion, and Ethnic Politics: Afghanistan, Iran, and Pakistan*, edited by Ali Banuazizi and Myron Weiner, 1–20. Syracuse, NY: Syracuse University Press.

Bisseret, Noëlle. 1979. *Education, Class Language, and Ideology*. London: Routledge.

Boggs, Carl. 1984. *The Two Revolutions: Antonio Gramsci and the Dilemmas of Western Marxism*. Cambridge: South End Press.

Brubaker, Rogers. 2005. "The 'diaspora' diaspora." *Ethnic and Racial Studies* 28 (1): 1–19.

Choi, Inbom. 2003. "Korean Diaspora in the Making: Its Current Status and Impact on the Korean Economy." In *The Korean Diaspora in the World Economy*, edited by C. Fred Bergsten and Inbom Choi, 9–30. Washington, DC: Peterson Institute.

Cenoz, Jasone, and Valencia Jose F. 1993. "Ethnolinguistic Vitality, Social Networks and Motivation in Second Language Acquisition: Some Data from the Basque Country." *Language, Culture, and Curriculum* 6 (2): 113–127.

Chopra, Pran N. 2003. *A Comprehensive History of India*. New Delhi: Sterling Publishers.

Clyne, Michael. 1982. *Multilingual Australia*. Melbourne: River Seine.

Cohen, A. P. 1985. *The Symbolic Construction of Community*. London: Tavistock.

Currie, Michael, and Michael A. Hogg. 1994. "Subjective Ethnolinguistic Vitality and Social Adaptation Among Vietnamese Refugees in Australia." *International journal of the sociology of language* 1994 (108): 97–116.

Cyprian, Eric. 1991. "A People without a Language." (*The News*, March 7). Islamabad, Opinion Page.

De Varennes, Fernand. 1996. *Language, Minorities and Human Rights*. London: Martinus Nijhoff.

Dei, George J. Sefa, and Shahjahan Riyad. 2008. "Equity and Democratic Education in Ghana: Towards a Pedagogy of Difference." In *Comparative and Global Pedagogies: Equity, Access and Democracy in Education*, edited by Joseph I. Zajda, Lynn Davies, and Suzanne Majhanovich, 49–70. London: Springer.

Dorian, Nancy C. 1980. "Language Loss and Maintenance in Language Contact Situation." In *The Loss of Language Skills*, edited by R. Lembert and B. Freed, 1–25. Rowley, MA: Newbury House.

Dorian, Nancy C. 1992. "Introduction." In *Investigating Obsolescence: Studies in Language Contraction and Death*, edited by Nancy C. Dorian, 1–12. Cambridge: Cambridge University Press.

Duong, Thanh. 2002. *Hegemonic Globalization: U.S. Centrality and Global Strategy in the Emerging World Order*. London: Ashgate.

Edwards, John R. 1985. *Language, Society, and Identity*. Oxford: Blackwell.

Fasold, Ralph. 1984. *The Sociolinguistics of Society*. Oxford: Blackwell.

Fishman, Joshua A. 1970. *Sociolinguistics: A Brief Introduction*. Rowley, MA: Newbury House.

Fishman, Joshua A. 1991. *Reversing Language Shift: Theoretical and Empirical Foundations of Assistance to Threatened Language*. Clevedon: Multilingual Matters.

Gal, Susan. 1979. *Language Shift: Social Determinants of Linguistic Change in Bilingual Austria*. Boston, MA: Academic Press.

Gardner, R. C. 1985. *Social Psychology and Second Language Learning: The Role of Attitudes and Motivation*. London: Edward Arnold.

Giles, Howard, Bourihis Richard, and D. M. Taylor. 1977. "Towards a Theory of Language in Ethnic Group Relations." In *Language, Ethnicity, and Inter-Group Relations*, edited by Howard Giles, Richard Bourihis and D. M. Taylor, 307–349. London: Academic Press.

Giles, Howard, and Rosenthal David. 1985. "Perceived Ethnolinguistic Vitality: The Anglo- and Greek-Australian Setting." *Journal of Multilingual and Multicultural Development* 6 (3–4): 253–269.

Holmes, Janet, and Ray, Harlow. 1991. *Threads in the New Zealand Tapestry of Language*. Auckland: Linguistic Society of New Zealand.

Husband, Charles, and Khan Verity Saifullah. 1982. "Some Viability of Ethnolinguistic Vitality: Some Creative Doubts." *Journal of Multilingual and Multicultural Development* 3 (3): 193–205.

Irfani, Suroosh. 2004. "Pakistan's Sectarian Violence: Between the "Arabist Shift" and Indo-Persian Culture." In *Religious Radicalism and Security in South Asia*, edited by Satu P. Limaye, Mohan Malik, and Robert G. Wirsing, 147–170. Honolulu, Hawaii: Asia-Pacific Center for Security Studies.

Korth, Britta. 2005. *Language Attitudes Towards Kyrgyz and Russian: Discourse, Education and Policy in Post-Soviet Kyrgyzstan*. Berlin: Peter Lang.

Kulick, Don. 1992. *Language Shift and Cultural Reproduction: Socialization, Self, and Syncretism in a Papua New Guinean Village*. Cambridge: Cambridge University Press.

Landry, R. and Allard R. 1994. "Diglossia, Ethnolinguistic Vitality and Language Behavior." *International Journal of the Sociology of Language* 108 (1): 15–42.

Levinson, David. 1998. *Ethnic Groups Worldwide: A Ready Reference Group*. Phoenix, AZ: The Orynx Press.

Li, W. L. 1982. "The Language Shift of Chinese Americans." *International Journal of the Sociology of Language* 1992 (38): 109–24.

Malik, Abdullah and Ahmad, Salim. 2004. *Masud Khaddarposh: Savanih Hayat* [Biography]. Lahore: Sang-e-Meel Publications.

Mann, Charles C. 2000. "Reviewing Ethnolinguistic Vitality: The Case of Anglo-Nigerian Pidgin." *Journal of Sociolinguistics* 4 (3): 458–474.

Mansoor, Sabiha. 1993. *Punjabi, Urdu, English in Pakistan: A Sociolinguistic Study*. Lahore: Vanguard.

McKenzie, Robert M. 2010. *The Social Psychology of English as a Global Language: Attitudes, Awareness and Identity in the Japanese Context*. London: Springer.

Meyerhoff, Miriam. 2006. *Introducing Sociolinguistics*. London: Routledge.

Mohiuddin, Yasmeen Niaz. 2007. *Pakistan: A Global Studies Handbook*. Santa Barbara, CA: ABC-CLIO.

Nadiem, Ihsan H. 2005. *Punjab: Land, History, People*. Lahore: al-Faisal Nashran.

Ndhlovu, Finex. 2009. *The Politics of Language and Nation Building in Zimbabwe*. Berlin: Peter Lang.

Phillipson, Robert. 1992. *Linguistic Imperialism*. Oxford: Oxford University Press.

Pieter, J. Fourie. 2001. *Media Studies: Institutions, Theories, and Issues*. Cape Town: Juta and Company Ltd.

Plaza, Sonia, and Ratha Dilip. 2011. "Harnessing Diaspora Resources for Africa." In *Diaspora for Development in Africa*, edited by Sonia Plaza and Dilip Ratha, 1–54. Washington, DC: World Bank Publications.

Qadeer, Mohammad A. 2006. *Pakistan: Social and Cultural Transformations in a Muslim Nation*. New York: Routledge.

Rahman, Tariq. 1996. *Language and Politics in Pakistan*. Karachi: Oxford University Press.

Rahman, Tariq. 2002. *Language, Ideology and Power: Language-Learning Among the Muslims of Pakistan and North India*. Karachi: Oxford University Press.

Rasinger, Sebastian M. 2007. *Bengali-English in East London: A Study in Urban Multilingualism*. Berlin: Peter Lang.

Reading, Anna. 1999. "Campaigns to Change the Media." In *The Media in Britain: Current Debates and Developments*, edited by Jane Stokes and Anna Reading, 170–182. London: Palgrave Macmillan.

Romaine, Suzanne. 1995. *Bilingualism*. Oxford: Blackwell.

Romaine, Suzanne. 2012. "Contact and Language Death." In *The Handbook of Language Contact*, edited by Raymond Hickey, 320–339. Oxford: John Wiley & Sons.

Saxena, Mukul. 1995. A Sociolinguistic study of Panjabi Hindus in Southall: Language maintenance and shift. Unpublished D.Phil. thesis, University of York.

Sayahi, Lotfi. 2005. "Language and Identity Among Speakers of Spanish in Northern Morocco: Between Ethnolinguistic Vitality and Acculturation." *Journal of Sociolinguistics* 9 (1): 95–107.

Schiffman, Harold F., and Spooner Brian. 2011. "Afghan Languages in a Larger Context of Central and South Asia." In *Language Policy and Language Conflict in Afghanistan and its Neighbors: The Changing Politics of Language Choice*, edited by Harold F. Schiffman, 1–28. Leiden: Brill.

Schweigkofler, Anny. 2000. "South Tyrol: Rethinking Ethnolinguistic Vitality." In *German Minorities in Europe: Ethnic Identity and Cultural Belonging*, edited by Stefan Wolff, 63–72. Oxford: Berghahn Books.

Shackle, Christopher. 2007. "Pakistan." In *Language of National Identity in Asia*, edited by Andrew Simpson, 100–115. Oxford: Oxford University Press.

Shah, Mehta Ali. 1997. *The Foreign Policy of Pakistan: Ethnic Impacts on Diplomacy 1971–1994*. London: I.B.Tauris.

Shuttleworth, Kate. 2012. "Agreement Entitles Whanganui River to Legal Identity." *The New Zealand Herald*, August 30. Accessed February 14, 2013. http://www.nzherald.co.nz/nz/news/article.cfm?c_id=1&objectid=10830586

Siapera, Eugenia. 2010. *Cultural Diversity and Global Media: The Mediation of Difference*. New York: John Wiley and Sons.

Singh, Shailendra Kumar. 2001. *Multilingualism*. New Delhi: Bahri.

Singh, Pritam. 2008. *Federalism, Nationalism and Development: India and the Punjab economy*. New York: Routledge.

Skutnabb-Kangas, Tove, and Phillipson Robert, eds. 1994. *Linguistic Human Rights: Overcoming Linguistic Discrimination*. New York: Mouton de Gruyter.

Taylor, Peter James. 1993. *Political Geography: World-Economy, Nation-State, and Locality*. London: Longman Scientific & Technical.

Tollefson, James. 1991. *Planning Language, Planning Inequality*. New York: Longman.

Wardhaugh, Ronald. 1986. *An Introduction to Sociolinguistics*. Oxford: Basil Blackwell.

Weinreich, Uriel. [1953] 1974. *Languages in Contact*. Berlin: Walter De Gruyter Inc.

West, Barbara A. 2009. *Encyclopedia of the Peoples of Asia and Oceania*. New York: Infobase.

Williams, Glyn. 1992. *Sociolinguistics: A Sociological Critique*. London: Routledge.

Wilson, John. 2009. "Preface." In *Pakistan: The Struggle Within*, edited by John Wilson, i–xxvi. New Delhi: Dorling Kindersley.

Wilson, Clint, and Felix, Gutierrez. 1985. *Minorities and Media: Diversity and the End of Mass Communication*. London: Sage.

Zaidi, Abbas. 2010. "A Postcolonial Sociolinguistics of Punjabi in Pakistan." *Journal of Postcolonial Cultures and Societies* 1 (3–4): 22–55.

Zaidi, Abbas. 2013. *Language shift: Sociolinguistic lives of two Punjabi generations in Brunei Darussalam*. Lahore: Classic Books.

(Dis)honourable paradigms: a critical reading of *Provoked, Shame* and *Daughters of Shame*

Shweta Kushal and Evangeline Manickam

Department of Humanities and Social Sciences, Indian Institute of Technology Madras, Chennai, India

The construction of an ethnic identity is based on the confluence of self and culture. Ethnic groups in the diaspora preserve ethnic identity by expecting adherence to communal and social codes and the Punjabi community in the UK is no exception. The construction of women as the repository of honour or *izzat* is the most important construct used to establish cultural order. This equates women with collective honour resulting in extreme psychological, mental and physical control over them. Therefore, they are unable to dissociate themselves from this construct and find themselves trapped within its confines. This paper locates *Provoked* by Kiranjit Ahluwalia and Rahila Gupta and *Shame* and *Daughters of Shame* by Jasvinder Sanghera in this context outlining the establishment and exertion of this construct, which perpetuates patriarchal order. It argues that the act of utterance through the autobiographies creates a space for alternative means of self-definition and presents counter-narratives to this hegemonic discourse.

Introduction

Cultural codes and their all-encompassing presence form the central tenets with reference to which identity is constructed in individuals. Cultural identity can be defined as an aspect of individual identity that is under direct influence of the community or the culture to which one belongs. In order to understand the manner in which ethnic consciousness functions in a community, it is important to understand how culture functions in creating this consciousness. In the essay 'Cultural Studies: Two Paradigms', Stuart Hall, through his discussion of Raymond Williams' *Long Revolution*, says that there are two ways of conceptualising 'culture'.

> The first relates 'culture' to the sum of the available descriptions through which societies make sense of and reflect their common experiences... the second emphasis is more deliberately anthropological, and emphasizes that aspect of 'culture' which refers to social *practices*.... 'culture is a whole way of life'. (Hall 1995, 196)

He further argues that '"Culture" is not *a* practice; nor is it simply the descriptive sum of the "mores and folkways" of societies ... It is threaded through *all* social practices, and is the sum of their inter-relationships' (Hall 1995, 197). In the domain of cultural studies, Hall argues that culture is signified by

> *both* the meanings and values which arise amongst distinctive social groups and classes, on the basis of their given historical conditions and relationships, through which they 'handle' and respond to the conditions of existence; *and* as the lived traditions and practices through which those 'understandings' are expressed and in which they are embodied. (Hall 1995, 199)

Punjabis, in a migrant environment, position themselves as an ethnic community with distinct awareness of class, race, language and religion. They become identifiable as an ethnic group due to the 'lived traditions and practices' exhibited in their unique attire, language, religion and cultural symbols. Eames and Robboy observe that 'The use of turbans by men and the use of Punjabi dress by women is related to their obvious self-identification as Punjabis' (1978, 211). Punjabis in the West, through this positioning, have created a niche for themselves in the adopted land and continue to observe their own cultural codes in a world with evidently different cultural systems. These distinctive markers grant cohesion to this group and allow for instant recognition of and by members belonging to the same group.

Elaborating on the theme of preserving cultural identity, in their discussion of Punjabis in Canada, Bhat and Sahoo point out that, Punjabis show a great degree of community cohesiveness. 'They visit each other, attend ceremonies, attend Gurdwara services and take community lunch programmes besides associations and organisations to promote the interest of community as a whole' (2003, 144). They further add that Punjabi migrants maintain strong sociocultural, economic, religious and political networks with their kith and kin around the world as well as with their relatives in Punjab. Elaborating on marriage and kinship ties, they observe, 'Punjabis uphold their social networks through family ties and kinship obligations, marriage ceremonies and other ritual activities. The family is the basis of social organisation, providing its members with both identity and protection' (Bhat and Sahoo 2003, 146).

Ethnic identity, however, relies heavily on this association of self and culture for its formulation and negotiation. The preservation of ethnic identity is carried out by strict adherence to certain communal and social codes that in turn propagate the cultural ethos of the group. Barot, Bradley, and Fenton (1999, 7) state that, 'ethnicity is a socially reproduced system of classification.' They further add that in this system of classification created by a population or a group, 'the categories are ... chosen rather than imposed; the bases of classification are principally culture, religion, language and ancestry; and equally they are related to collective and individual memories and current lives' (Barot, Bradley, and Fenton 1999, 8). This construction of a social ethnic classification results in the formation of groups which may become communities 'by having a real basis of shared life, grounded in region or locale, reproduced through kinship and the social reproduction of cultural forms' (Barot, Bradley, and Fenton 1999, 9). In the context of the Punjabi community, these 'cultural forms' are rituals and communal practices. Eames and Robboy (1978) delineate methods employed by Punjabis living in Wolverhampton to maintain their ethnic identity. They observe,

> In interaction with others, both Punjabi and non-Punjabi, the individual is immediately identified as a member of the community through a number of observable manifestations. The most immediate of these consists of physical markers which include skin color, style of dress and culturally based mannerisms. (1978, 211)

These work as symbolic representations of ethnic identity. They add that 'Punjabis tend to limit their meaningful social interaction to other Punjabis' (Eames and Robboy 1978, 218). However, having taken into account the above observations, the present paper argues that the most important construct used to establish cultural order is that of honour or *izzat* where the woman is the repository of this ever-fragile and prime aspect of social identity. This equating of the woman with familial or social honour results in extreme control over the women of the community because of which they are unable to imagine life outside this construct. This paper locates *Provoked* by Kiranjit Ahluwalia and Rahila Gupta and *Shame* and *Daughters of Shame* by Jasvinder Sanghera in this context and examines this glorified construct of honour to delineate its social purpose of absolute control over the women which fortifies the typically patriarchal structure of this ethnic group. These texts are autobiographical in nature and outline the experience of the women of the diasporic Punjabi community in the UK.

Patriarchy, ethnicity and the Punjabi community

One of the major aspects of the Punjabi community is that it is largely patriarchal in nature. Hartmann defines patriarchy as, 'a set of social relations between men, which have a material base, and which, though hierarchical, establish or create inter-dependence and solidarity among men that enable them to dominate women' (Hartmann 1979, 8). Millett states,

> If one takes patriarchal government to be the institution whereby that half of the populace which is female is controlled by that half which is male, the principles of patriarchy appear to be twofold: male shall dominate female, elder male shall dominate younger. (1977, 25)

Patriarchal control extends to all spheres of human life and controls dominant ideology. As a result, most ideals regarding human beings are generated in order to fuel this dominance. Brown and Jordanova point out that

> The idea that biological differences between men and women cause social ones is, of course, extremely pervasive, and it has gained prominence through the recent spate of writings on socio-biology. Earlier we called it a dominant ideology. Now we want to argue that it is grounded in Western thought, and especially in science, medicine and technology; hence its dominance. (1995, 513)

This argument that dominance is gained because of grounding in Western thought hints at the insidious manner in which cultural and social paradigms function. Patriarchal society and its systems of knowledge generation construct a dominance of the male principle over the female. The debate of the 'cultured male' and the 'natural female' has been explored by Sherry B. Ortner. She argues against biological determinism thus, '... not that biological facts are irrelevant, or that men and women are not different, but that these facts and differences only take on significance of superior/inferior within the framework of culturally defined value systems' (Ortner 1995, 495). According to Ortner, culture is the context in which biological differences achieve relevance.
Brown and Jordanova argue that

> Allowing the male value system to prevail was ... an integral part of the process of developing culture with which nature, raw and unmediated, would be controlled ... Women, as

nature were to be controlled, or rather channelled into the correct role for nature in the history of the human race. (1995, 514)

This role is characterised by the prominence of women in the domestic unit and their presence as its primary representatives. Women are charged with the task of 'the conversion of nature into culture, especially with reference to the socialization of children' as 'Any culture's continued viability depends upon properly socialized individuals who will see the world in that culture's terms and adhere more or less unquestioningly to its moral precepts' (Ortner 1995, 505). In diasporic communities, ethnic identity and its propagation and preservation become the responsibility of the women. They are required to act as custodians of ethnicity because, in a migrant condition, ethnicity plays out more in the realm of the community or the home which in turn is the domain of the women. 'Within many ethnic populations, women can be seen as having an important role as carriers of ethnicity, both in terms of ancestry (some communities have strict rules about intermarriage) and culture' (Barot, Bradley, and Fenton 1999, 15). Barot et al. discuss the stress that Yuval-Davis places on the role of 'symbolic boundary maintenance' which 'is enacted in a very concrete way as women simultaneously "embody" ethnic culture and gender: Women in their "proper" behaviour, in their "proper" clothing embody the line which signifies the collectivity's boundaries' (cited in Barot, Bradley, and Fenton 1999, 15). Therefore, the physical fact of a woman's body is marked with the boundaries that symbolise ethnicity and cultural codes. This places a distinct responsibility on the shoulders of the women of the community as 'it is in the home that cultural rules and practices are transmitted to the next generation, through the switchboard of the home that networks of ancestry and kinship are maintained' (Barot, Bradley, and Fenton 1999, 15). The 'female task of ethnicity maintenance' (Barot, Bradley, and Fenton 1999, 15) charges women with passing on the tenets of the community to future generations, more rigorously to girl children, in order to ensure compliance and propagation of the cultural heritage. 'When ethnic relations are played out in a minority context as a result of migration, women often may contribute to ethnicity maintenance in a more material way' (Barot, Bradley, and Fenton 1999, 15). The idea of shame and dishonour that may be brought upon the family if there are any transgressions also controls the behaviour of the women. Ethnicity then becomes controlling, hegemonic and does not allow any space to the members of the community, especially women, to express or exercise any difference from the norm.

Izzat and the female body: social control vs. narrative intervention

Provoked, *Shame* and *Daughters of Shame* are autobiographical narratives of two women, both Punjabi migrants in the UK, which provide an alarming picture of the community to which they belong. These narratives question the construction of social honour that curbs and controls women of this community. *The Circle of Light*, now popularly known as *Provoked*[1] after the movie, is the story of Kiranjit Ahluwalia, the woman who, in the year 1989, became a household name in the UK because of burning her husband alive following 10 years of a physically, emotionally and mentally abusive marriage.[2] The narrative is a life history which covers the significant event of her marriage to a British citizen, Deepak Ahluwalia, 10 years of abuse in that marriage, her murder of her husband through burning and her ultimate release from prison after serving time for her crime. Kiranjit Ahluwalia is a first-generation migrant who was born in the Chakkalal region of Punjab in India. She moved to the UK only after her marriage to Deepak in the year 1979 and stayed in Crawley, West Sussex, with him. *Shame* is Jasvinder Sanghera's autobiography that tells the tale of her mother disowning her when she runs away from home, at the age of 14, for fear of a forced marriage. Jasvinder is a second-generation migrant who has never known any other place as home. She is a British citizen, born and raised in the derby county of the developed country. Both these women have lived in different parts of the UK but their experience of the ideal of honour and its dominance over their community is similar. Through this reading, it becomes obvious that the tenet of honour and its accompanying norms are uniformly observed by subsections of the Punjabi diasporic community in the UK. In *Daughters of Shame*, Jasvinder Sanghera relates the experiences of other women of this diasporic community she comes in contact with through her support organisation, Karma Nirvana. These women have undergone similar or worse treatment at the hands of their families. They belong to Muslim, Sikh and Hindu communities that have shared cultural norms because of their collective past and shared territory before and during the partition of British India. The reality of a collective past for these communities before the Independence of India results in cultural similarities that continue to exist even across national borders and in spite of migration to the West. Ethnic identities constructed in this manner predate and consequently subsume national identities that came into force post-Partition. This classification of community is ethnic and regional in nature rather than being religious or national. These three texts are all autobiographical narratives that depict the diasporic Punjabi community with a strong sense of *izzat*.

Izzat cannot be explained adequately by its English equivalent 'honour' as it is an amalgam of honour, dignity, prestige and social position. Honour/*izzat* as a concept has been widely interpreted through centuries and across societies in order to lay down acceptable behaviours for a community. Brandon and Hafez describe this concept and its various aspects thus:

> At various times honour has been equated with attributes as diverse as bravery or cunning, strength or wisdom, vengefulness or mercy. In all societies, honour has both a private and a public aspect. On one hand it describes an individual's 'self-respect'; how a person sees himself and his relative value in society. But at the same time, measures of honour also dictate the extent to which society accepts a person's self-worth and help determine the level of status and material benefits which it accords him as a result. (2008, 3)

This is the broad definition and association of the term 'honour' as understood across human interactions and societies. It is important to note that even in this broad classification, honour is directly linked with self-worth, status and material benefits that an individual may hope to derive from it. The addition of a sexual dimension to this results in a potent amalgam capable of fuelling passions. Michel Foucault in his *History of Sexuality* discusses the manner in which sex and sexuality are used in the public domain to construct a discourse of control. He shows how 'sex and sexuality move from being private, pleasurable, sociocultural interactive practices into medical, juridical, and moral/ethical discourses of disease, control, and reproduction' (Munns and Rajan 1995, 84). The construction of what Brandon and Hafez call 'Sexual Honour' works precisely to exercise control by converting the private realm of women's sex and sexualities into a concern of social, ethnic and public formulation of communal identities. Brandon and Hafez describe this 'Sexual Honour' stating that it is based on

> ... ideas that the reputation and social standing of an individual, a family or a community is based on the behaviour and morality of its female members. Like other forms of honour, this concept does not exist in a vacuum but rather as a central part of a complex social structure which governs relationships between different families, genders and social units within a given society. (2008, 3)

The Punjabi ethnic community attaches honour to the sexual and social behaviours of the women of the community. This practice extends beyond national borders into diasporic communities as well. Roger Ballard discusses the reasons for the migrants' maintenance of familial and social structures that were observed in the home land.

> Most migrants have made great efforts to sustain the unity of their families, both because this proved an excellent way of coping with their economic circumstances, and also because this was perceived as a most effective bastion against the corrosive influence of British culture. (Ballard 1982, 7)

This continued formulation of honour then becomes a central part of the self-definition of the diasporic Punjabi community. According to this view, female 'honour' becomes the currency that is used to measure the worth and social standing of the entire family and any deviation from the honour ideal is dealt with severely. Through the practice of dowry exchange at weddings, women's bodies and sexuality acquire a monetary value which encourages men of the family to guard them as they would any other capital. According to Ladislav Holy, 'honour is a similar resource to property, economic cooperation or power. It too has to be secured and protected in the same way as these other resources' (cited in Brandon and Hafez 2008, 4).

Women's responsibilities as the primary carriers of ethnic and cultural symbols lead to further controls as the 'stability of the domestic unit as an institution must be placed as far as possible beyond question' (Ortner 1995, 505) in order to ensure proper socialisation of its members. As women are the primary agents of this socialisation, they tend to come under heavier restrictions and controls which ensure unpolluted continuation of cultural codes. In their discussion of the growth of honour as the central tenet of social behaviour, Brandon and Hafez comment that men have been able to 'embed ideas of honour in culture by asserting their right to be the civil, political and economic leaders of society at the expense of women' (2008, 4). Further,

> men's ability to uphold these ideas of 'proper' female behaviour and ensure that women conformed to these social norms became equated with their own social standing, status and 'honour'. Upholding the honour of men and women therefore became dependent on restricting women's actions, behaviour and thoughts. (Brandon and Hafez 2008, 4)

Ortner discusses these mechanisms of control as being inherently embedded in the cultural systems that define the domestic unit as the woman's domain. She states that in patriarchal cultures, 'her [woman's] permissible sexual activities are more closely circumscribed than man's, she is offered a much smaller range of role choices, and she is afforded direct access to a far more limited range of its social institutions' (Ortner 1995, 505). Ortner highlights that the social construction of womanhood only cements this control and ensures compliance.

> Further, she is almost universally socialized to have a narrower and generally more conservative set of attitudes and views than man, and the limited social contexts of her adult life reinforce this situation. This socially engendered conservatism and traditionalism of woman's thinking is another – perhaps the worst, certainly the most insidious – mode of social restriction, and would clearly be related to her traditional function of producing well-socialized members of the group. (Ortner 1995, 505)

This requirement to produce 'well-socialised members of the group' results in close monitoring and scrutiny of women's actions which are directly linked to *izzat*. Further, it makes women more stringent followers and enforcers of ethnic norms. Jasvinder Sanghera's mother in *Shame* is an example of how women internalise and enforce communal norms. She constantly impresses upon her daughters that it is their duty to 'uphold the good name of the family. That is the very least that your father and I expect' (Sanghera 2007, 22). Actions that will endanger the *izzat* of the family are to be avoided. This is echoed in an encounter that Jasvinder has as a child when 'a man had flashed at me and Robina on the way home from school. My mild-mannered dad was furious and he raged at us: "You must avoid these situations, do you want to bring dishonour on yourself?"' (Sanghera 2007, 223) As a result the woman or the girl-child has a 'belief that she brought his cruelty on herself' (Sanghera 2007, 222). A girl-child or a woman must always 'avoid situations' even when they are completely out of her control. Ballard discusses the importance of *izzat* in the Punjabi community. He observes that

> ... honour accrues to the family as a group, and not just to individual males within it, the advancement of their corporate *izzat* is one of the most important goals which South Asian families set themselves. The maintenance of *izzat* depends both upon the family's wealth and its members' conformity with ideal norms of behaviour; but it is advanced most effectively by arranging prestigious matches for the family's daughters, and by outshining its rivals in the gift exchanges which take place at such events. (Ballard 1982, 5)

The *izzat* ideal that is constructed on the basis of the sexual behaviours of women and through 'members' conformity with ideal norms of behaviour' is further advanced through prestigious matches for daughters. These matches are possible only when the girl's character, her sexual and social behaviour, is beyond reproach. The practice of reciprocal gifting at these high-profile wedding events further heightens the collective *izzat* of the family. Jasvinder Sanghera's *Shame* discusses this idea of prestigious matches through Jasvinder's mother's horror at her daughter's actions. In the prologue of *Shame*, Jasvinder describes calling her mother after having run away from home to avoid a forced marriage. Although she calls her parents in the hope that their voice will 'ring with pleasure and relief' and that they will tell her to 'Stay right where you are, *putt* (my child), we're coming to get you' (Sanghera 2007, 2), the reality could not be further from this hope. On making the call, Jasvinder's experience is far removed from this dream of hers.

> She [her mother] was off straight away, screaming and crying down the phone, and the voice I'd yearned to hear was harsh and shrill. 'What have you done to us? How could you do this? You've shamed us. Why should we suffer this disgrace?' (Sanghera 2007, 2)

Concern for the daughter and her well-being is obliterated in the horror of losing honour. While the parents could have advanced their *izzat* through a suitable match for their daughter, Jasvinder has utterly shamed them by running away with a boy from a lower caste. She has tarnished the *izzat*, not only by breaking the ideal norms of behaviour but also by associating her high-class and upper-caste *jat*[3] family with a low-class and low-caste *chamar*.[4] While Jasvinder's actions are a great blow to the *izzat* of her family, even minor 'deviation from the ideal norms' is not tolerated by ethnic communities as it is necessarily 'the first step on the slippery slope towards wholesale Anglicization. The slightest lapse thus seems to indicate total disloyalty' (Ballard 1982, 5) in this community. As 'izzat is at stake', it becomes

> imperative for every family to participate in the game of status competition if they do not wish to fall behind. The consequent necessity for every family member to maintain an impeccable and honourable reputation is a thoroughgoing constraint on everyone's behaviour. (Ballard 1982, 7–8)

Jasvinder's actions then signify the ultimate transgression of ideal norms. Owing to all these reasons, it has become imperative for women to follow the norms laid down with this honour ideal in mind in order to avoid heaping shame upon their families. The inextricability of honour and shame that arises from dishonour creates a stronghold on the women of the community. The primacy of honour in their lives becomes so internalised that they are unable to transgress these boundaries even in extreme circumstances.

Kiranjit Ahluwalia's situation, as outlined in *Provoked*, is one such extreme circumstance. Living in an abusive marriage where she is treated as property by her husband, she has no means to avoid her situation. All her pleas to leave Deepak over the years after being married to him go unheard. It is acceptable for a woman to undergo unthinkable abuse if that will assure her continued marital status and preserve the social façade that the family has constructed over the years. A woman in Kiranjit's situation has very limited choices.

> If I became single again, the old burden of being a burden to my family would come back to haunt me. I would be accused by my community of being a woman without character. These chains of character, divorce, *izzat*, family were tying me down. (Ahluwalia and Gupta 2008, 95)

In *Provoked*, Kiranjit gives a detailed description of what an 'ideal woman' is supposed to be in her society. In her speech for her campaign, she delineates the features that an ideal woman is required to possess.

> In order to uphold this false 'honour' and glory, she is taught to endure many kinds of oppression and pain in silence. In addition, religion also teaches her that her husband is God and fulfilling his every desire is her religious duty. A woman who does not follow this path in our society has no respect or place in it. She suffers from all kinds of attacks and much hurt entirely alone. She is responsible not only for her husband but for his entire family's happiness. (Ahluwalia and Gupta 2008, 243)

The speech clearly highlights that culture, religion and society together form a psychological, social, emotional and physical stronghold on the women of this community. Any deviation from these established boundaries and frameworks results in social ridicule and ostracism. The means of escaping oppression are limited and, when explored, the social setup and family step in to curtail that rudimentary initiative. Kiranjit says that 'I also tried several times to escape from the trap of my anguished married life. But each time, my husband and family put pressure on me, in the name of upholding their *izzat*' (Ahluwalia and Gupta 2008, 243). Ballard points out that in South Asian families,

> Divorce is seen as a last resort, to be adopted only when other remedies fail. For a woman remarriage is not an attractive proposition. It spells dishonour, both for herself and her family, and she is unlikely to be able to obtain a well endowed groom. (1982, 9)

Since this 'last resort' is unlikely to generate options for a better future, women like Kiranjit find it increasingly difficult to escape their wretched lives. 'Given the enormous difficulties and disadvantages that permanent departure from the family almost invariably entails, it is obviously worthwhile making every possible effort in identifying and achieving an internal renegotiation of relationships' (Ballard 1982, 11). Kiranjit continues to try and achieve this renegotiation but is ultimately pushed to the brink to exert herself in the act of killing her husband. The life that she lives with Deepak only results in depression due to her experiences of abuse and violence and she sees no way out of her situation. On the evening when she killed her husband, he tried to break her ankles and threatened to burn her face with a hot iron after she refused to give him money. She was consumed with rage and once Deepak was asleep, she mixed caustic soda in petrol and set his feet on fire. Bindel in her article quotes her as follows:

> I couldn't see an end to the violence... I decided to show him how much it hurt. At times I had tried to run away, but he would catch me and beat me even harder. I decided to burn his feet so he couldn't run after me. (2007)

This is the mental state in which she finally gives way to self-preservation and consequent self-affirmation.

In *Shame*, Jasvinder paints a picture of how honour works and the manner in which its importance is made clear at a very early age of a girl's life.

> If an Asian girl went out with a white boy that was different, that was bad. Her brothers or her uncles would find him and beat him up and then they would beat her too, for bringing shame on the family. Then she would be ruined; no decent Asian man would ever want her. Everyone in the community knew that. I knew it when I was eight. No one handed me a book of rules but I knew the particular way in which I was supposed to act, walk, talk, even breathe. I knew that with every bad word said a reputation could die. (Sanghera 2007, 8)

The code of honour is passed on silently and girls learn it at an early age. They are aware that honour crimes or beatings are common, which in turn helps in reinforcing the code. Jasvinder highlights the manner in which all aspects of life are governed by the principle of honour. While it is unacceptable for a girl to be seen with a white boy, she is also not allowed to have a boyfriend who belongs to the Asian community. 'In the Asian community lots of girls and boys have to hide their romance' (Sanghera 2007, 55). Girls are not supposed to be seen in the company of boys irrespective of the race. Jasvinder learns this when she starts going out with Jassey, an Asian boy, and tells her mother about it. Her mother is aghast as is evident from her response, 'My daughter, *my daughter*, has a boyfriend. You have ruined yourself, girl. What will become of you? What will become of me? You have brought dishonour on us all' (Sanghera 2007, 61). For her mother, it is a personal affront and dishonour to have a daughter with a boyfriend, as evident from the emphasis she places on 'my daughter'. She feels that in spite of all her teachings her daughter has failed to grasp the significance of honour and this is a measure of her failure as a mother.

Jasvinder further describes how the system of honour teaches girls and women to accept any kind of atrocities and abuse. Jasvinder's sisters experience domestic violence in their married lives and reach out to their mother for help. Jasvinder witnesses her mother's response to these requests. The mother asks them to endure it as it is their 'duty to look after your husband and to please him' (Sanghera 2007, 21). Once married, the girls have to try and make a successful marriage as even the discussion of divorce or separation could bring shame to the family. The mother advises her daughters, 'It is your duty to have a respectable marriage ... Do you understand that?' (Sanghera 2007, 22). This vision haunts Jasvinder later when talks of her marriage are ripe. She is unable to look at her imminent marriage favourably.

> In all the hours I'd lain on my bed I'd been tormented by a vision of me and the man in the photograph sitting side by side on a settee while Mum lectured us about honour. In my mind's eye my face was bruised and there were tears pouring down my cheeks. (Sanghera 2007, 63)

Jasvinder knows that her mother will not offer any comfort and that she will be expected to bear everything in the name of honour. As the narrative progresses, Jasvinder relates her realisation that the only thing her parents care about is *izzat* and any price can be paid in order to safeguard it. 'As far as my mum and dad were concerned, personal happiness wasn't important. What mattered to them was having a daughter who was dutiful and respectable and did nothing to disgrace the family name' (Sanghera 2007, 139). Jasvinder's sister, Robina, feels that she has to make her marriage work because she has chosen Baldev. 'She had to prove to the community that she could make their union work as well as an arranged marriage' (Sanghera 2007, 139). Robina makes it very clear that 'If I left Baldev now, the shame would kill them' (Sanghera 2007, 139), because they had only just recovered from the dishonour that Jasvinder's running away from home had heaped upon them. As discussed earlier, *Provoked* also reflects this phenomenon where the women of the family are willing to put up with any kind of abuse in order to protect the honour of the family. Kiranjit lives a life of extreme physical, emotional, psychological and sexual torture for 10 years in order that her family and brothers do not have to bear the taint of dishonour.

Unfortunately, this safeguarding leads to tragedy as the women do not see a way out of this situation. While in *Provoked*, Dr. Merrill's report (Ahluwalia and Gupta 2008, 281) discusses the heightened tendency of Asian, specifically Punjabi, women to commit suicide by burning in the face of the odds and due to lack of options, Robina's suicide by burning in *Shame* is the lived reality of the same statistics. The structure of the community Robina belongs to hinders any act of self-preservation and leaves her trapped in her situation. The close-knit nature of the community ensures surveillance and scrutiny that would result in shame if she were to leave her husband. It does not offer any support. She is repeatedly told that she has no place, no position without her husband. It is shameful to be without him and this shame will, in turn, be heaped upon her family. She is emotionally blackmailed into accepting her situation through this threat.

> All she'd wanted was for the rows to stop and to have some reassurance that she would be supported by her family. What she was getting was reinforcement of all her worst fears from a man of stature, a man who was speaking for the people she loved, and the whole community where Mum and Dad had to live. (Sanghera 2007, 143)

The narrative in *Shame* relates many accounts in which honour is considered the most important thing and has to be upheld even when the physical, emotional and mental safety of a child is at stake. Ayesha, one of the many women Jasvinder comes in touch with through the work she does at Karma Nirvana, the organisation Jasvinder establishes to help victims of forced marriages without means of helping themselves, suffers the worst kind of abuse for many years and her mother refuses to help her. Ayesha is repeatedly raped by her brother and uncle since she was eight. When she plucks up the courage to tell her mother, the response she gets is shocking and shattering for the child.

> My Mum slapped my face. She said, 'Don't you dare disgrace this family. Cry at the bottom of the garden if you must, but don't bring your fuss in here'. My brother must have known she said that, because he stopped being careful, he did it more and more. (Sanghera 2007, 212)

Family name and honour are more important than the child and her safety or even her sanity. She is to be 'protected' from the men outside as she is the symbol of the family honour and ironically this task is usually performed by the brothers and uncles in a family. However, there is no avenue where she can seek safety or even help when the same people become the predators. She is thoroughly victimised and there is no forum to which she can turn for assistance. Ayesha continues to suffer abuse even after marriage, this time physical in nature, at the hands of her husband and when she goes 'sobbing to her mother' she is asked 'to be mindful of the family name and stop complaining' (Sanghera 2007, 212). All the abuse suffered by her is a private matter to be kept behind closed doors and no help should be sought outside lest it bring shame and dishonour.

In *Daughters of Shame*, Jasvinder recounts the stories of many women who have suffered forced marriages and honour-based crimes. These women belong to Muslim, Sikh and Hindu communities originally from the Punjab region, as it existed before the partition of India, and are now living in the UK. It tells harrowing tales of atrocities perpetrated by family members in the name of honour. Jasvinder, in discussing the women who approach her organisation for support says, 'the women who came to us for help were suffering honour-based violence – appalling cruelty meted out by whole family, not just by their husbands – and forced marriage' (Sanghera 2009, 9). These are tales of confinement, mistrust, threats and crimes. There are instances where a father is ready to kill and maim his own child in order to ensure that she does not cause dishonour to him and his family, and Fozia's story is one such example. Fozia comments on her father's treatment of her sister when she refuses to marry as per his wishes.

> Then suddenly my dad pinned Raveeda up against the wall and held a knife to her throat – I don't even know where he got that knife from, he must have had it hidden in his clothing – but he was shouting and yelling, and saying he would kill Raveeda if she didn't go through with it. (Sanghera 2009, 19–20)

Fozia says that he was the milder of her two parents but he was willing to go to any lengths to have his daughter follow the traditions and customs of his community because if she refused to do so, it would bring shame to his family. Fozia has been a witness to this violent nature of her father and realises that honour is the most important thing in life. Through this display, her father has ensured that not only one, but all his daughters learn the importance of this dictum. Killing a child is preferable to her bringing dishonour to the family and her father makes it very plain. 'I'd rather a daughter dead and myself in the prison than stand here and let the shadow of dishonour settle on my family' (Sanghera 2009, 22). The text also talks about mothers willing to subject their girls to any kind of abuse in order to have them uphold the honour of the family, as seen in Kiren's case. Kiren succeeds in running away from a forced marriage to the home of a 'sympathetic' uncle who calls her parents immediately. After she is taken home, Kiren's mother warns her about the treatment she will receive if she tries anything of this sort again.

> The first thing was, Mum held a knife to my throat and she was like, 'I'll cut your tongue off.' Then I went upstairs and they followed me and my stepdad was beating me up and my mum was shouting at me, she said, 'If you don't listen to us and do what we say, your stepdad is going to rape you'. (Sanghera 2009, 55)

Getting her own daughter raped is acceptable for her mother as long as it ensures obedience thereby saving their *izzat*. Ironically, *izzat* does not get defiled if this abominable act is performed by one member of the family on another.

The two protagonists of these narratives, however, engage in a construction of identity that rejects this overpowering construct through their basic urges for self-preservation. Kiranjit Ahluwalia's murder of her husband and Jasvinder Sanghera's elopement are both actions that render these women into outsiders who then question the validity and even the relevance of a social construct that spells extreme danger for these idealised members of the community.

Conclusion

The three texts analysed in this paper reveal the monstrous face of honour as experienced by the women of the Punjabi community in the UK. The idealising of women as the repository of family and communal honour becomes an instrument of complete control and abuse of the women of the community – psychologically, emotionally, even physically. This larger-than-life construct that epitomises and places the woman on a pedestal of purity traps her by depriving her of agency, individuality and self. The only way in which she can escape this predicament is through death – whether of self or the other – or through abnegation of self. Kiranjit Ahluwalia's murder of her husband may be an extreme act but it creates an avenue in which she can exercise self-assertion and can wrest the controls of her being away from society. Jasvinder Sanghera's decisive act of running away from home and then the proactive setting up of Karma Nirvana allow her to exist outside hegemonic forms of self-definition such as the honour rhetoric. Kiranjit Ahluwalia and Jasvinder Sanghera, through their narratives, raise a voice that subverts and attempts to overthrow the grand narrative of honour. The act of utterance through the autobiographies that they engage in creates a space for the existence and articulation of the self. The 'pedagogical discourse' of the construction of honour as the principal tenet of society is challenged in the articulation of the voice of the women who are marginalised by this discourse. This voice functions as a 'substantial intervention into those justifications of modernity – progress, homogeneity, cultural organicism, the deep nation, the long past – that rationalize the authoritarian, "normalizing" tendencies within cultures in the name of the national interest or the ethnic prerogative' (Bhabha 1990, 4). In so doing, the authors not only confront the homogenising impulse of the dominant discourse but also show how this voice is heard from within the very space that witnesses its discrimination and exclusion from the pedagogic origins of an ethnic community. They, therefore, question and rework the boundaries that mark a community's selfhood by demonstrating how 'counter-narratives' to the dominant discourse of ethnicity 'continually evoke and erase its totalizing boundaries – both actual and conceptual – disturb(ing) those ideological manoeuvres through which "imagined communities" are given essentialist identities' (Bhabha 1994, 149). These narratives exist very much within the 'performative' realm of the same community. While, for the women of the community, this space of articulation generates options of life that are not restricted by the honour–patriarchy–ethnicity triumvirate, these utterances also function as a call for action for the community to 'make honour really honourable' (Sanghera 2009, 285).

Notes

1. *Provoked* is a 2007 UK-based film that was inspired by Kiranjit Ahluwalia's autobiography, *Circle of Light*. The popularity of the movie has resulted in post-production editions of the text to be titled as *Provoked*. Further, Kiranjit Ahluwalia's case, known in British legal textbooks as R v Ahluwalia, changed the definition of the word 'provocation' in cases of battered women, which reclassified her crime as manslaughter instead of murder. This paper uses the nomenclature *Provoked* for the discussion of the text in order to draw attention to this change in definition in the legal system. However, there are no references to the feature film of the same name.
2. Kiranjit Ahluwalia was married to Deepak Ahluwalia at the age of 23, in the year 1979. After 10 long years of an abusive relationship in which she suffered physical violence, food deprivation, confinement and marital rape, she burnt her husband alive. He suffered severe burns over 40% of his body and died 10 days later as he developed complications and sepsis. Due to his death, Kiranjit Ahluwalia was arrested and charged with murder. She was sentenced to life imprisonment at Lewes Crown Court on 7 December 1989. At that time, her counsel failed to emphasise the severe violence she had endured and her mentally unstable condition in court. The intervention of the Southall Black Sisters on her behalf resulted in an appeal on the case as they continued to press for a mistrial. Her conviction was overturned in the year 1992 on the grounds of insufficient counsel and was replaced with manslaughter.
3. *Jat* is an upper caste in Sikhs.
4. *Chamar* is a prominent caste in India, Pakistan and Nepal. It is a Dalit sub-caste mainly found in the northern states of India such as Punjab, Haryana, Himachal Pradesh, Uttar Pradesh, Bihar and Delhi. The traditional occupation of this caste was processing, manufacturing and trading in leather and leather goods. Due to their association with tanning, they have had a low social status traditionally. They are still considered as untouchables in some parts of India.

References

Ahluwalia, K., and R. Gupta. 2008. *Provoked: The Story of Kiranjit Ahluwalia*. New Delhi: Harper Collins.

Ballard, R. 1982. "South Asian Families: Structure and Process." In *Families in Britain*, edited by R. Rapoport, M. Fogarty and R. Rapoport, 179–204. London: Routledge. Accessed January 8, 2012. http://www.casas.org.uk/papers/pdfpapers/families.pdf

Barot, R., H. Bradley, and S. Fenton, eds. 1999. *Ethnicity, Gender and Social Change*. London: Macmillan.

Bhabha, H. K. 1990. *Nation and Narration*. London: Routledge.

Bhabha, H. K. 1994. *Location of Culture*. London: Routledge.

Bhat, C., and A. K. Sahoo. 2003. "Diaspora to Transnational Networks: The Case of Indians in Canada." In *Fractured Identity: The Indian Diaspora in Canada*, edited by S. J. Varma and R. Seshan, 141–167. New Delhi: Rawat Publications.

Bindel, J. 2007. "I Wanted Him to Stop Hurting Me." *The Guardian*, April 4. Accessed July 14, 2012. http://www.guardian.co.uk/world/2007/apr/04/gender.ukcrime

Brandon, J., and S. Hafez. 2008. *Crimes of the Community: Honour-Based Violence in the UK*. London: Centre for Social Cohesion.

Brown, P., and L. Jordanova. 1995. "Oppressive Dichotomies: The Nature/Culture Debate." In *A Cultural Studies Reader: History, Theory and Practice*, edited by J. Munns and G. Rajan, 509–519. London: Longman.

Eames, E., and H. Robboy. 1978. "The Wulfranian and the Punjabi: Conflict, Identity and Adaptation." *Anthropological Quarterly* 51 (4): 207–219.

Hall, S. 1995. "Cultural Studies: Two Paradigms." In *A Cultural Studies Reader: History, Theory and Practice*, edited by J. Munns and G. Rajan, 194–205. London: Longman.

Hartmann, H. 1979. "The Unhappy Marriage of Marxism and Feminism: Towards a More Progressive Union." *Capital and Class* 3 (2): 1–33.

Millett, K. 1977. *Sexual Politics*. London: Virago.

Munns, J., and G. Rajan, eds. 1995. *A Cultural Studies Reader: History, Theory and Practice*. London: Longman.

Ortner, S. B. 1995. "Is Female to Male as Nature Is to Culture?." In *A Cultural Studies Reader: History, Theory and Practice*, edited by J. Munns and G. Rajan, 491–508. London: Longman.

Sanghera, J. 2007. *Shame*. London: Hodder & Stoughton.

Sanghera, J. 2009. *Daughters of Shame*. London: Hodder & Stoughton.

Index

A Postcolonial People: South Asians in Britain. Ali, Nasreen, Kalra, Virinder S and Sayyid, Salman 49
Abbas, Riffat *see* Sufi influence in the works of Siraiki Poet, Riffat Abbas
Adeney, Katherine 77
Afghanistan, occupation of 7
Ahluwalia, Kiranjit 3, 89–90, 93–4, 96, 98
Akbar, Mughal emperor 2, 19
Ali, Fateh 43, 46
Ali, Mubarek 43, 46
Ali, Nasreen 49
Ali, Tariq 9
Allard, Real 75
Alvi, Hamza 76, 78
American Realism 55
An American Brat. Sidhaw, Bapsi 9, 14, 19, 20
Anarkali's Tomb 19
Ansari, Sarah FD 61
Appadurai, Arjun 15
Arab Spring 21
Arabist shift 80–1
art 9, 12–14
Arts and Humanities Research Council-led Connected Communities Research Programme 28
Aurangzeb, Mughal emperor 6
Australia: ethnic Maltese 74; Vietnamese refugees 75
authenticity 36–7, 44, 46
Axel, Brian Keith 1–2

Baba Farid Gunj Shakar 56
Badshahi mosque 2, 6, 9–10, 14
Bahawalpur, Princely State of 61
Baker, Colin 73, 80
Ballard, Roger 92–5
Baluchi language 73
Bangladesh, secession from Pakistan of 6, 81
Banuazizi, Ali 77
Barker, Clare 20
Barot, Rohit 88, 90
Basti Sheikh 43–4
Bhanga Moves. Roy, Anjali

bhangra music and dancing 33, 36–7, 45–6, 48, 50
Bhardwaj, Ajay 50–1
Bhat, Chandrashekhar 88
Bhatra Sikhs 29
bifurcation of Punjab, demands for 64, 67, 69
bin Laden, Osama 81
Bindel, Julie 95
biological determinism 89
Birmingham, England 32–3, 35, 36–7, 47–8
Black Atlantic 25
Bollywood 42–3, 46, 47
Bourihis, Richard 73–4, 75
Bradley, Harriet 88
Brandon, James 91
Brown, Louise 9–10
Brown, Penelope 89–90
Brutus, Dennis 67–8
BS Balli Qawwal Paslewale group 51
Burney Abbas, Shemeem 60

Canada, community cohesiveness in 88
caste: dalits 46; gender 93–4; *izzat* (honour), notion of 93–4; *jat* caste 46, 94; *Kanjari* caste 9; *Khatri* business caste 46; *Punjabiyat* 42–3, 46; Sikhs 46; United Kingdom, Little Punjabs of 26
censorship 7
chamar caste 93
Chandan, Amarjit 9
children, socialization of 90
Chinese Americans and language 74
chronotopes 17
Cities and Citizenship. Holston, James and Appadurai, Arjun 15
class: Lahore in novels of Bapsi Sidhaw and Mohsin Hamid 8, 20; Punjabi language in Punjab, diasporification of 74–7, 83; Siraiki poet, Riffat Abbas, Sufi influence on 58, 62–3
Clifford, James 37
Clyne, Michael 74
Cocoo's Den 9–11
cognitive mapping 17, 21
Cold War 7

INDEX

colonialism: India 2, 6–7; Khan, Nusrat Fateh Ali, music of 43, 46; Lahore in novels of Bapsi Sidhaw and Mohsin Hamid 6, 15–17, 20, 21; megacities 2; postcolonialism 2, 6–7, 15, 20, 21, 66, 68, 80; Punjabi language in Punjab, diasporification of 72, 76, 80–1; Punjabi village and villagers as colonial construct 2; Siraiki poet, Riffat Abbas, Sufi influence on 55, 57, 61, 66, 68–9
Cracking India. Sidhaw, Bapsi 6, 13–16, 20
The Crow Eaters. Sidhaw, Bapsi 15
culture: collective past 91; definition 87–8; dress 88; ethno-cultural construct, Punjab as 2; folk culture 56, 58, 66–8; gender 91–2, 94, 98; homeland 2, 25; identity 87–8; Khan, Nusrat Fateh Ali, music of 45–9; Lahore 6–8, 13–15, 17–18; language 56–8, 63, 69; patriarchy 89–90; Punjabi language in Punjab, diasporification of 74–5, 78; *Punjabiyat* 42–3, 45–9; shocks 24–5; Siraiki poet, Riffat Abbas, Sufi influence on 56–69; United Kingdom 24–5, 35–7, 47–9; youth culture 32, 35–7, 48–9
Currie, Michael 75
Cyprian, Eric 81

Dagar Bani of Dhrupad 46
dalits 46
Dalrymple, William 7
dancing girls of Lahore 9–10, 13–15
Data Darbar Sufi shrine, attack on 8
Daughters of Shame. Sanghera, Jasvinder 3, 89–91, 97
Davis, Ray 8
de Certeau, Michel 7, 19–21
Dei, George J. Sefa 74
Delhi, India 18
democracy 76
demography 73, 76, 77–8, 80
Deobandi Muslims 10
Desai, Anita 9
dervishes 60
Dhrupad music 46
diasporification of Punjabi language in Punjab 71–83: attitudes towards language, Punjabi's 80–2; class 74–7, 83; colonialism 72, 76, 80–1; culture 74–5, 78; demography 73, 76, 77–8, 80; discrimination 72; economic domination 73–5, 77, 78; education 74–5, 79, 80–1; Ethnolinguistic Vitality Model (EVM) 73–82; gender 75; identity 3, 72, 82; institutional support 73–6, 78–9, 81; Language Maintenance/Language Shift (LMLS), or Language Shift (LS) 73; language shift 73, 79–80; marginalization 72–3, 80; marriage between ethnicities 77–8; media 74, 78, 81; migration and emigration 74, 77, 80; Pakistan 72–83; religion 78–9, 80; Sikhs 76; sociohistorical status 74; sociolinguistics 72–3, 75, 78–80, 82; status 73–4, 76, 80
diglossia 78–9
Dis-Orienting Rhythms. Kaur, Raminder and Kalra, Varinder 49
divorce 94–6
DJ Ritu 50
domestic violence 90–1, 95–8
Dornyei, Zoltan 75
dowry exchange 92
dress 15, 20, 50, 59, 88
drone killings 8
Dudrah, Rajinder 26
Dunia media house 78

Eames, Edwin 88
East Africa, migrants from 26, 33
economic domination 73–5, 77, 78
education 74–5, 79, 80–1
essentialism 3, 99
ethnic identity: gender 88–92, 98–9; Khan, Nusrat Fateh Ali, music of 45–6; Lahore in novels of Bapsi Sidhaw and Mohsin Hamid 8, 17; Punjabi language in Punjab, diasporification of 3, 72, 81; Siraiki poet, Riffat Abbas, Sufi influence on 643, 66; women as enforcers of ethnic norms 90, 93, 98
Ethnolinguistic Vitality Model (EVM) 73–82
European Commission Seventh Framework Research Programme 28

Faislabad (Lyallpur), Pakistamn 44–5, 47
Faiz, Faiz Ahmed 8, 67
Faiz Ghar 8
Faqir, Alan 56
Farid, Khwaja Ghulam 3, 55–68
Farina, Mir 43
Fasold, Ralph 80
Fenton, Steve 88
fiction *see* Lahore in novels of Bapsi Sidhaw and Mohsin Hamid
film industry 42–3, 46–7
Finney, Nissa 27
Fishman, Joshua A 81–2
folk culture 56, 58, 66–8
food 6, 29–30, 33, 36–7
forced marriages 91, 93, 97–8
Foucault, Michel 6, 15, 17–18, 91

Gabriel, Peter 48
Gal, Susan 80
Gardner, Robert C 80
Gaur, Ishwar 42, 45
gender 87–99: caste 93–4; control 89–98; culture 91–2, 94, 98; dancing girls of Lahore 9–10, 13–15; *Daughters of Shame*. Sanghera,

INDEX

Jasvinder 3, 89–91, 97; divorce 94–6; domestic violence 90–1, 95–8; enforcers of ethnic norms, women as 90, 93, 98; equality 56, 60–1; ethnic identity 89–92, 98–9; *izzat* (honour), notion of 3, 89–98; *Kafis* 61; killing of husband 90–1, 95, 98; Lahore in novels of Bapsi Sidhaw and Mohsin Hamid 8, 13–14, 20; marriage 93–8; patriarchy 3, 89–90, 92, 98; prostitution 2, 6, 9–11, 13–15, 18, 20, 21; *Provoked*. Ahluwalia, Kiranjit and Gupta, Rahila 3, 89–90, 93–4, 96, 98; *Punjabiyat* 51; religion 91, 94, 97; rural Punjabi norms 3, 92; self-alienation 20; sexual honour 91–3; *Shame*. Sanghera, Jasvinder 3, 89, 91, 93–8; Siraiki poet, Riffat Abbas, Sufi influence on 56, 60–1; social construction of womanhood 92–3; social control versus narrative intervention 90–8; suicide by burning 96; United Kingdom, diasporic community in 25, 89–99

geographies of Punjabiness 26–8, 37
Ghana, minority languages in 74
ghazals 13–14, 56, 65
Ghosh, Amitav. *The Shadow Lines* 18
Giles, Howard 73–4, 75
Gill, Harjant Singh 27
Gilmartin, David 2
Gilroy, Paul 25
Glover, William 17, 19
God 57–62, 64–5, 68
Google 'Reunion' advert 5–6
Graded Intergenerational Disruption Scale (GIDS) 81–2
Gupta, Rahila 3, 89–90, 93–4, 96, 98
gurdwaras 29, 31–5, 47, 88

Hafez, Salam 91
Hall, Stuart 87–8
Hamid, Mohsin, novels of 2, 5–21
Handsworth, England 36–7, 47
Hans, Hans Raj 41–2
Harlow, Ray 80
Hartmann, Heidi 89
Hashmi, Salima 8–9
Heer Ranjha 47, 49, 58–9
Heera Mandi. Le Tournier D'Ison, Claudine 10
Heera Mandi, red light district of 2, 6, 9–11, 13–15, 18, 20, 21
heterotopia 17–18
Hindi 29, 56
Hindus 9, 43, 76, 91, 97
hippie trail 7
History of Sexuality. Foucault, Michel 91
Hogg, Michael A 75
Holmes, Janet 80
Holston, James 15
Holy, Ladislav 92
homeland: culture 2, 25; diasporic construct, as 2; framing device 25; imagined homeland 1–2; loyalty 25; originary homeland 3, 25, 37; return, notion of 25, 27–8, 37; Siraiki poet, Riffat Abbas, Sufi influence on 56–7, 59–61; United Kingdom, Little Punjabs of 25, 37

honour *see izzat* (honour), notion of
Hounslow, England 33, 35, 36–7
How to Get Filthy Rich in Rising Asia. Hamid, Mohsin 11, 20
human rights 72
Husband, Charles 75
Hussain, Iqbal 7, 9, 12

identity: authenticity 46; caste 26, 36; culture 87–8; Khan, Nusrat Fateh Ali, music of 42, 45–6, 50; migrants 88; myths 2; narratives 1; religion 26, 32, 34–6, 42–7, 49, 51; Siraiki poet, Riffat Abbas, Sufi influence on 56, 58, 60–1, 68–9; United Kingdom, Little Punjabs of 25–7, 32, 34–6 *see also* ethnic identity
imagined communities 99
Imperial Eyes. Pratt, Mary Louise 15
India: colonialism 2, 6–7; democracy 76; gender 51; Hindus 43, 76; independence 7, 16–17, 91; Khan, Nusrat Fateh Ali, music of 46, 50–1; Lahore in novels of Bapsi Sidhaw and Mohsin Hamid 6–7, 16–17; multilingualism 75; Muslims 76, 81; nuclear standoff of late 1990s 7, 16; post-colonialism 6–7; pre-colonial India 6; *Punjabiyat* 42–3, 50; Sikhs 76; Siraiki poet, Riffat Abbas, Sufi influence on 69; United Kingdom 25–37
indigenous/native languages 72
industrialization 21, 80
Iqbal, Allama 44
Iqbal Fellows at Oxford and Cambridge University 43
Iqbaliat Qawaali 44
Iranian Revolution of 1979 7
Irfani, Suroosh 80
Ishq-e-Haqiqi 58–9
Ishq-e-Mujazi 58–9
Islam *see* Muslims
izzat (honour), notion of: definition 91; gender 3, 89–98; sexual honour 91–3; shame 93–7

Jabbar, Naheem 14
Jacoviello, Stefano 44
Jameson, Fredric 6, 17
Jang/Geo media house 78
Jashn-e-Farid 67
jat caste 46, 94
Jat Sikhs 2, 46
Jeevan Jog 56
Jehan, Noor 8
Jinnah, Muhammad Ali 7
Jordanova, Ludmilla 89–90

INDEX

Kafis 3, 55–69: The *Kafi* Movement 56, 66, 68; modern *Kafis* 55, 57, 61–9; pantheist philosophy in Farid's *Kafis* 57; traditional *Kafis* 55–61, 63–4; women 61
Kalra, Varinder S 25, 49
Kanjari caste 9
Karma Nirvana 91, 97, 98
Kaur, Raminder 25, 49
Khalistan, proposal for 43
Khan, Ayub 47–8
Khan, Behram 46
Khan, Nichola 27
Khan, Nusrat Fateh Ali *see Punjabiyat* and music of Nusrat Fateh Ali Khan
Khan, Pathanay 56
Khan, Rahat Fateh Ali 41, 49
Khatri business caste 46
Khushal Khan Khattak 56
Khyber Pakthunkhwa (ex-Northwest Frontier Province) 7
Kinna Sohna 50
Kipling, Rudyard 9
Korth, Britta 74
Kulick, Don 80

Lacan, Jacques 18
Lahore in novels of Bapsi Sidhaw and Mohsin Hamid 5–21: *An American Brat*. Sidhaw 9, 14, 19, 20; art 9, 12–14; Badshahi mosque 2, 6, 9–10, 14; class 8, 20; colonialism 6, 15–17, 20, 21; *Cracking India*. Sidhaw 6, 13–16, 20; *The Crow Eaters*. Sidhwa 15; cultural capital of Pakistan, Lahore as 7–8; culture 6–8, 13–15, 17–18; dancing girls 9–10, 13–15; ethnic divisions 8, 17; fundamentalists and liberals, chasm between 8, 9–10, 14; gender 8, 13–14, 20; Heera Mandi, red light district of 2, 6, 9–11, 13–15, 18, 20, 21; hippie trail 7; *How to Get Filthy Rich in Rising Asia*. Hamid 11, 20; India 6–7, 16–17; international machinations 7–8; Lawrence Gardens 16–17; migration from rural areas 8–9, 11–12; *Moth Smoke*. Hamid 9, 13, 16, 20; 'Mughal City of Gardens' 2; nostalgia 6, 18; *The Pakistani Bride*. Sidhwa 15; partition 5–7, 9, 16; rural areas 8–9, 11–12; *The Reluctant Missionary*. Hamid 18–19; space in theory and imagination 15–21; terrorist target, Lahore as 8; time 15; urbanization 10–13, 15–20; violence 7, 16; walking 19–21; Walled City 14, 20
Landry, Rodrigue 75
Language Maintenance/Language Shift (LMLS), or Language Shift (LS) 73
languages: Baluchi 73; culture 56–8, 63, 69; ethno-linguistic construct, Punjab as 2; Hindi 29, 56; Khan, Nusrat Fateh Ali, music of 42–3; multilingualism 75; Persian 49–50, 56; Punjabi 29, 31, 33–4; *Punjabiyat* 9, 42–3, 46, 50–1, 57; Sindhi 56, 73, 79; Siraiki 56–8, 63, 68, 73; Urdu 56, 65, 73, 79, 81–2; *see also* diasporification of Punjabi language in Punjab
Lapierre, Dominique 7
Lasoori Shah, shrine of 44
Le Tournier D'Ison, Claudine. *Heera Mandi* 10
Lefebvre, Henri 16
Lesbian, Gay and Transgender South Asian club nights 50
Levitt, Peggy 25
Li, Wen Lang 74
Lieven, Anatol 8, 17
liminal space 18
Little Punjabs of UK 2–3, 24–37: authenticity 36–7; British Punjabi, identification as 26; caste identity 26, 36; culture 24–5, 35–7; double consciousness 34; gender 25; geographies of Punjabiness 26–8, 37; homeland 25, 27–8, 37; identity 25–7, 32, 34–6; India 25–37; inner cities, move away from 27; life histories 3, 24, 26, 28–37; loyalty 25; multiple place attachments 28; nostalgia 3, 25; Punjabi 29, 31, 33–4; Punjabiness 35–7; racism 30; religious identity 26, 32, 34–6; return, notion of diasporic 27–8, 37; second generation 3, 24–5; Sikhs 26, 28, 30–7; Southall Broadway 3, 24–6, 30–1, 35–7; Thandi coach route maps 3, 26–8; visits and trips 24–7, 29–30, 32, 35–7; youth culture 32, 35–7; White towns and cities 27–36
Lok Geet (folksongs) 56
Lok Virsa Institute, Islamabad 45, 46
Lollywood industry 8–9
London, England 47–50
Long Revolution. Williams, Raymond 87–8
loyalty 25
Lyallpur (Faislabad), Pakistan 44–5, 47

Magic Touch album. Khan, Nusrat Fateh Ali 48, 50
majoritarianism 72–3
Malhotra, Anshu 43, 46
Maltese in Australia 74
Manto, Saadat Hasan 9
marginalization 72–3, 80
marriage: divorce 94–6; dowry exchange 92; ethnicities, between 77–8; forced marriages 91, 93, 97–8; gender 93–8; *izzat* (honour), notion of 93; Punjabi language in Punjab, diasporification of 77–8
Marsden, Magnus 27
Marxism 81
media 7, 74, 78, 81
Melas 49

INDEX

metropolitan/hinterland dynamic 2
Meyerhoff, Miriam 75
migration and emigration: East Africa, migrants from 26, 33; identity 88; partition 7, 82; Punjabi language in Punjab, diasporification of 74, 77, 80; rural areas to Lahore, from 8–9, 11–12; second generation 24; Transnet or Transnationalisation, migration and transformation research project 28
Millett, Kate 89
Minar-e-Pakistan 14
Mir, Farina 43, 46, 47
Mirror Stage 18
Mohiuddin, Yasmeen Niaz 78
Moth Smoke. Hamid, mohsin 9, 13, 16, 20
Mueenuddin, Daniyal 9
Multan, Pakistan 56, 64–5, 67
muhajits (migrants and descendants) 7
multiple place attachments 28
Mumbai Fables. Prakash, Gyan 15
Musharraf, Pervez 7
music 56, 64, 67 *see also* Punjabiyat and music of Nusrat Fateh Ali Khan
Muslim League 44
Muslims: Badshahi mosque 2, 6, 9–10, 14; culture 91; Deobandi Muslims 10; fundamentalists and liberals, chasm between 8, 9–10, 14; gender 51; India 76, 81; Islamization 81; *izzat* (honour), notion of 97; Khan, Nusrat Fateh Ali, music of 42; Punjabi language in Punjab, diasporification of 80; *Punjabiyat* 51; Shi'a 10, 14 *see also* Sufi influence in the works of Siraiki Poet, Riffat Abbas; Sufis
Myron, Weiner 77
mysticism (*tasawwuf*) 56–62, 66, 68
myths 2

Nabi, Farjad 44
Nagra, Daljit 9
National Festival of Asian Music 49
nationalism 1, 6, 45–6, 63
The Nation's Tortured Body. Axel, Brian Keith 2
naturalism 66
Ngugi Wa Thiongo 67–8
Ni mai jana jogi de naal 41–2
Nizamuddin Auliya 43, 44
nostalgia 3, 6, 18, 25, 42–3
novels *see* Lahore in novels of Bapsi Sidhaw and Mohsin Hamid
nuclear standoff between India and Pakistan 7, 16
Nur-ud-din Mohammad Salim, Mughal Emperor 19

Oriental Star Agencies 47–8
Ortner, Sherry B 89, 92–3

Pakistan: Bangladesh, secession of 6, 81; censorship 7; dominance of Punjabis 77; gender 51; Islamization 81; Khan, Nusrat Fateh Ali, music of 43, 46, 50–1; nuclear standoff of late 1990s 7, 16; Punjabi language in Punjab, diasporification of 72–83; Siraiki poet, Riffat Abbas, Sufi influence on 69; Urdu 82; West, relations with 7
Pakistan: A Hard Country. Lieven, Anatol 8
The Pakistani Bride. Sidhwa, Bapsi 15
Pandey, Gyanendra 6
pantheist philosophy 57
Paradise Club, East London 50
Parsi community 14–15
partition 1947: collective past 91; Google 'Reunion' advert 5–6; Hindus 97; Khan, Nusrat Fateh Ali, music of 43–7, 50–1; Lahore in novels of Bapsi Sidhaw and Mohsin Hamid 5–7, 9, 16; Muslims 97; *Punjabiyat* 50–1; Sikhs 97; Siraiki poet, Riffat Abbas, Sufi influence on 57, 69; Urdu speakers, migration of 82; violence 6
Parveen, Abida 56
Pashto 56, 73, 79
Patar, Surjit 50
patkas 30, 34
patriarchy 3, 89–90, 92, 98: biological determinism 89; definition 89; domestic unit, role of women in 90, 92; socialization of children 90
Persian 49–50, 56
Peterborough 28–31: Millfield 29–30; Orton Longueville 30
Places for all? A multi-media investigation of citizenship, work and belonging in a fast-changing provincial city 28
poetry *see* Sufi influence in the works of Siraiki Poet, Riffat Abbas
police 20
Postcolonial Spaces. Teverson, Andrew and Upstone, Sara 15
postcolonialism 2, 6–7, 15, 20, 21, 66, 68, 80
Prakash, Gyan. *Mumbai Fables* 15
Pratt, Mary Louise. *Imperial Eyes* 15
Princely State of Bahawalpur 61
Pritam, Amrita 9
Progressive Writers Association 8
prostitution 2, 6, 9–11, 13–15, 18, 20, 21
Provoked. Ahluwalia, Kiranjit and Gupta, Rahila 3, 89–90, 93–4, 96, 98
Punjab Reconsidered. Malhotra, Anshu and Mir, Farina 43
Punjabi: Khan, Nusrat Fateh Ali, music of 49; Siraiki poetry 56; United Kingdom, Little Punjabs of 29, 31, 33–4 *see also* diasporification of Punjabi language in Punjab; *Punjabiyat*
Punjabiness 3, 26–7, 35–7

INDEX

Punjabiyat: Bollywood 46; caste 42–3, 46; culture 42–3; definition 9, 43; gender of performers 51; India 42–3; Muslims 51; nation 42, 51; nostalgia 51; Pakistan 42–3; partition 50–1; religious identity 42–3, 51; Sikhs 42–3, 46; Siraiki poet, Riffat Abbas, Sufi influence on 57 *see also Punjabiyat* and music of Nusrat Fateh Ali Khan

Punjabiyat and music of Nusrat Fateh Ali Khan 41–51: authenticity 44, 46; body 45–6; Bollywood 42–3, 47; colonialism 43, 46; culture 45–9; diaspora 3; ethnicity 45–6; film tracks 42–3, 47; framing of *Punjabiyat* 50; generational cross-over 48; identity 42, 45–6, 50; India 46, 50–1; instruments, shift in 46; *Kinna Sohna* 50; language 42–3; London 47–50; *Magic Touch* album 48, 50; musical continuity 3, 43, 46; Muslims 42; nation 45–6; Pakistan 43, 46, 50–1; partition 43–7, 50–1; Persian language 49–50; Qawaali music 41–9, 51; religious identity 44–7, 49; world music 43, 47–8; youth subculture 48–9

Qadeer, Mohammad A 78
Qawaali music 41–9, 51
Qureshi, Regula 45

racism 30
Radio Pakistan 44
Randhawa, Balwant (life history) 31–3
Rasinger, Sebastian M 75
Reading, England 31–3, 36
realism 57–63, 65–7
religion: gender 91, 94, 97; God 57–62, 64–5, 68; gurdwaras 29, 31–5, 47, 88; identity 26, 32, 34–6, 42–7, 49, 51; Lahore in novels of Bapsi Sidhaw and Mohsin Hamid 6; parallel piety 47; Punjabi language in Punjab, diasporification of 78–9, 80; *Punjabiyat* 42–3, 51; Qawaali music 44–5; sectarianism 7; Siraiki poet, Riffat Abbas, Sufi influence on 56, 57–9, 61, 65–5, 68; United Kingdom, Little Punjabs of 26, 32, 34–6; Zoroastrianism 14 *see also* Muslims; Sufi influence in the works of Siraiki Poet, Riffat Abbas

The Reluctant Missionary. Hamid, Mohsin 18–19
return, notion of 25, 27–8, 37
Robboy, Howard 88
Rogaly, Ben 28
Rohi desert 59–61, 64, 67
Romaine, Suzanne 80
romanticism 66
Roy, Anjali. *Bhangra Moves* 45
Rumi 62
rural areas 2, 3, 8–9, 11–12, 92
Rushdie, Salman. *The Satanic Verses* 12

Sabri-Chisti order 44
Sachal Sarmust 57
Saeed, Fouzia 14
Sagoo, Bally 48, 50
Sagoo, Sa, 48
Sahoo, Ajaya Kumar 88
Saifullah, Khan Verity 75
Sair-ul-Urooj (upward march towards god) 57
Sakata, Hiromi Lorraine 44–5
Sanghera, Jasvinder 3, 89–91, 93–8
Sani, Tina 8
Sarangi 46
The Satanic Verses. Rushdie, Salman 12
Saxeni, Mukul 75
Sayyid, Salman 49
scholarship, boundaries and borders in 43
Schweigkofler, Anny 75
Scotland, language campaigns in 74
second generation Punjabis 3, 24–5
sectarianism 7
September 11, 2001 terrorist attacks 21
sexual honour 91–3
Shackle, Christopher 2
The Shadow Lines. Ghosh, Amitav 18
Shah Abudul Latif Bhitai 56, 62
Shah, Bulleh 41, 42, 56–7, 62
Shah Hussain 56
Shahjahan, Riyad 74
Shahmukhi script 51
shame 93–7
Shame. Sanghera, Jasvinder 3, 89, 91, 93–8
Sharif, Nawaz 81
Shenai 46
Shi'a Muslims 10, 14
Sidhaw, Bapsi, novels of 2, 5–21
Shiv Kumar Batalvi (song) 51
Shukla, Sandhya 25–6
Sikhs: caste 46; hegemony 43; India 76; *izzat* (honour), notion of 97; Jat Sikhs 2, 46; nationalism 45–6; partition 97; Punjabi language in Punjab, diasporification of 76; *Punjabiyat* 42–3, 46; Sikh and Punjab studies 1; United Kingdom, Little Punjabs of 26, 28, 30–7; United States, Sikh studies Chairs in 43
Simpson, Ludi 27
Sindhi 56, 73, 79
Singh, Dalip, maharaja 76
Singh, Jazz (life history) 33–6, 37
Singh, Khushwant 9
Singh, Malkit 48
Singh, Pritam 76
Singh, Ranjit 15
Singh, Ron (Rupinder) (life history) 24–5, 28–31, 33
Singh, Shailendra Kumar 75
Singh, Surinder 42, 45
Siraiki 2, 56, 73 *see also* Sufi influence in the works of Siraiki Poet, Riffat Abbas

INDEX

social class *see* class
social construction: gender 92–3; Punjab as a social construct 1, 2
social morphology 1
sociolinguistics 72–3, 75, 78–80, 82
Sohni Mahiwal 49
Soho Road, Birmingham 3, 32–3, 37
Soja, Edward M 6, 15–17
Soviet Union 7
space 2, 11–12, 18, 25
spirituality 56–62, 65, 67
Sri Lankan cricket team, attack on 8
state of consciousness, Punjab as 1, 2
The State of Islam. Toor, Saadoa 9
Steel, Flora Annie 9
stream of consciousness 62–3
Sufi influence in the works of Siraiki Poet, Riffat Abbas 3, 55–69: apprehension and insecurity 63–4; bifurcation of Punjab, demands for 64, 67, 69; British rule, resistance against 61, 68–9; class 58, 62–3; colonialism 55, 57, 61, 66, 68–9; culture 56–69; disconnection between modern and traditional *Kafis* 57; division of Punjab, opposition to 57; ethnicity 63, 66; Farid, Khwaja Ghulam 3, 55–68; female protagonists 56, 58, 60–1; folk culture 56, 58, 66–8; gender equality 56, 60–1; God 57–62, 64–5, 68; identity 56, 58, 60–1, 68–9; imagery 56, 61–3, 65–7; *Kafis* 3, 55–69; linguistic culture 56–8, 63, 69; love, spiritual and physical 56, 58, 60–2, 65; modern *Kafis* 55, 57, 61–9; motherland 56–7, 59–61; Multan 56, 64–5, 67; music 56, 67; mysticism (*tasawwuf*) 56–62, 66, 68; nostalgia 63; pantheist philosophy in Farid's *Kafis* 57; paradoxes and ambiguities 59, 64; partition 57, 69; political themes 60–1, 64, 65–9; *Punjabiyat* 57; realism 57–63, 65–7; religion 56, 57–9, 61, 65–5, 68; revision of Sufi imagery 65–6; rulers and ruled, mediators between 61; spirituality 56–62, 65, 67; state, resistance against the 56; stream of consciousness 62–3; symbolism 56, 60, 63–4, 67–8; traditional *Kafis* 55–61, 63–4, 66–9; urbanization 64, 67
Sufis 8, 42–5, 48, 50 *see also* Sufi influence in the works of Siraiki Poet, Riffat Abbas
suicide by burning 96
symbolism 56, 60, 63–4, 67–8

Tala Sharif, near Dasua, Hoshiarpur 44
Talbot, Ian 2, 13
Taliban 8, 81
Taseer, Salman 8
Taylor, Donald M 73–4, 75
terrorism 8, 19

Teverson, Andrew 15
Thandi coach route maps 3, 26–8
time 15
Toor, Saadia. *The State of Islam* 9
Transl-Asia 25, 37
translocalism 25, 28
transnationalism 1, 28
Transnet or Transnationalisation, migration and transformation research project 28
Tully, Mark 7

United Kingdom: gender 89–99; Iqbal Fellows at Oxford and Cambridge University 43; musical culture 47–9 *see also* colonialism; Little Punjabs of UK
United States: Afghanistan, involvement of 7; barriers to movement 19; Chinese Americans and language 74; Cold War 7; drone killing 8; nostalgia 6; Sikh studies Chairs 43; World Trade Centre attacks 19
Upstone, Sara 15
urbanization 10–13, 64, 67, 80
Urdu 56, 65, 73, 79, 81–2
Urs of Data Sahib, Lahore 45

Vertovic, Steven 1
Vietnamese refugees in Australia 75
violence: domestic violence 90–1, 95–8; drone killings 8; Lahore in novels of Bapsi Sidhaw and Mohsin Hamid 7, 16; partition 6; sectarianism 7

Wahadat-ul-Wajood 57
Walder, Dennis 6
Wales, language campaigns in 74
walking 19–21
Waqt media house 78
Wardhaugh, Ronald 78
Waris Shah, Peer Syed 57–8
Wasda Rahey Punjab Facebook site 51
Waters, Mary C 25
Weinreich, Uriel 80
West, Barbara A 77
Williams, Glyn 75
Williams, Raymond. *Long Revolution* 87–8
Wilson, John 7
women *see* gender
world music 43, 47–8
World Trade Centre attacks 19

youth culture 32, 35–7, 48–9
Yuval-Davis, Nira 90

Zee TV 48–9
Zia-ul-Haq, Muhammad 7, 9, 81
Zimbabwe, minority languages in 74
Zoroastrianism 14